D1130261

THE ILLEGAL
TRIAL OF CHRIST

THE ILLEGAL
TRIAL OF CHRIST

STEVEN W. ALLEN
ATTORNEY AT LAW

*May all your trials
lead you closer to Christ.*

Legal Awareness Series, Inc.
Mesa, Arizona

Published by Legal Awareness Series, Inc.
1550 E. McKellips Road, Suite 111
Mesa, Arizona 85203

ISBN: 1-879033-31-3

Printed in the United States of America

ABOUT THE COVER PICTURE

The cover picture is entitled "Ecce Homo" (the Latin and Italian words for "Behold the Man") painted by Antonio Ciseri (1821–1891). It is on display at the Hennepin Avenue Methodist Church in Minneapolis, Minnesota. It was the first painting to be given to the church, around 1900.

It has been said that Pontius Pilate had great interest in gladiators, having himself received training in hand-to-hand combat. Because of this, he was an avid follower of the Olympic Games. In the days of Pilate, the Olympics were held annually in Rome, and it was the gladiator slaves who participated. In an heroic effort to emerge final victor, each gladiator would fight for his life in each day's mortal combat. He who survived the ten-day ordeal was proclaimed the winner, or "Ecce Homo."

When the Emperor placed a garland of olive branches on the winner's head and pronounced him the new "Ecce Homo," he became a free man and an officer in the Emperor's royal guard.

Twice during the trial of Jesus, Pilate pronounced him "not guilty." The Jews protested loudly and threatened rebellion. Pilate, on probation from Tiberius Caesar for having allowed rebellion on two prior assignments, knew he could not afford to allow a third. Stepping closer to Christ before pronouncing judgment, Pilate better observed the broken, bleeding body of Jesus. Perhaps the garland of thorns circling Christ's head reminded Pilate of the many Roman gladiators of the past who had triumphed and been crowned victors.

As Pilate studied Jesus once again, he declared the words every gladiator longed to hear, "Ecce Homo—Behold the Man!" From Pilate, at least, Christ received his due acknowledgment.

Everett Penrod, *Pilate: Victor or Victim?* (Kearney: Morris Publishing, 2002) Cited in Donna Nielsen, *Reading Between the Lines: Mining the Treasures of Scripture* (Provo: Onyx Press, 2004).

TABLE OF CONTENTS

Acknowledgments

As a young attorney I was asked by a church leader to give a lecture to a group of adult Christians about the Trial of Christ from a Lawyer's Standpoint. Against my protestations, a time for the presentation was set and I was granted several months for research and preparation. My first presentation was candidly not very good. It did, however, lead to additional requests for repeat presentations to new audiences. This led to more study, research, and pondering on my part. This continued study has been a matter of wonder and awe in my life. For nearly three decades now my study has been more meaningful, my research more focused, and my presentation has evolved. So I thank that first church leader for his initial invitation, his patience, and his confidence.

The requests to put the information shared at my presentations into book form have become more persuasive and have increased in persistence. I was finally convinced to give it a try. I turned to my friend and editor, Rosemary Green, for her assistance. She has taken my sometimes convoluted notes, disjointed outlines, and rudimentary book drafts and through her care, close attention, and long-suffering has turned them into this book.

In the midst of her editing, she has had her own thoughts and inspirations which have become a part of this volume. At the very time she was revising the words about Christ's sacrifice for us, when returning to college her own daughter was killed in a tragic automobile accident. In addition to Rosemary's overwhelming grief over this loss, she came to understand more completely and intimately Christ's extraordinary and selfless sacrifice for each of us—and for her personally. This calamity added a new dimension to Rosemary's already faithful and painstaking care with words, thoughts, and feelings. She literally gave part of herself to the completion of this book.

For her grief, I am sincerely heavy-hearted. For her assistance with this book I am eternally grateful. Thank you, Rosemary.

ONE

INTRODUCTION

*Acts 8:25 "And they, when they had testified
and preached the word of the Lord . . . "*

J esus Christ *did* walk Judea. But this book isn't intended to
prove that point; history itself proves that Christ lived. Instead,
this book discusses the illegal trial that led to the completion of
his ultimate sacrifice. This book is for those who already recognize the saving divinity of Jesus Christ. It is for those who *know*.
And those who *believe*. And those who simply *hope* that the
miracle of Jesus is real.

Christ's trial was a mockery of Jewish law. Ironically, those
who violated that law throughout the trial were the very people
entrusted with *making* and *enforcing* the law—with *preventing*

injustice. Understanding their brazen violation of law adds a new dimension to the tragedy of the trial and the cross, inspiring a more appreciative love for Christ and his humble endurance.

In further irony, the actions of these ancient lawmakers help prove the *truth* of Jesus Christ's divinity. Terrified of his mission, deeds, and power to expose their misconduct, and condemned by the simple truth of his words, they sought to preserve their power and wealth by destroying the man before his teachings could destroy them.

They began by concocting half-truths and lies to defame him. Then they judged him, breaking many of their own laws in the process. Finally, they connived to put him to death in the most heinous manner of their time.

But in killing Christ, their plot backfired. Instead of putting an end to his teachings, they fulfilled all prophecy pertaining to his death. Their scheming and law-breaking *did* place Jesus on the cross, but his suffering ensured that the simple carpenter became the Savior of the world, of all mankind. The Savior of even those very men who were instrumental in his death.

This book contributes to our understanding of Christ's mission by examining the laws broken by the rulers of the time. Understanding that the trial of Christ was in reality four separate trials—two Hebrew and two Roman—makes this miscarriage of justice even more barbaric, because laws were broken at all four trials.

As I have traveled the country speaking on this topic, my audiences have shared with me two concerns about my subject. First, some people claim that we have no accurate, concurrent, or contemporary record describing the rules of law during Christ's trial. However, we do have records describing Hebrew and Roman law of a period some years after this trial, and laws are not prone to change radically over short periods of time. (In the United States, for example, most of our Constitutional principles have been followed for over 200 years.) It seems that each of the Gospel writers have noticed or mentioned certain details that were important to them. Is there any other reason for the writers to include these details other than to illustrate that certain laws should have been followed? At the time Christ was brought before the Sanhedrin, nearly every criminal rule that applied can be traced to Mosaic provisions which had been in place for more than 1,000 years. Those rules in all probability would not have been developed in the single generation between the fall of Jerusalem when it was conquered by Pompey the Great in 63 B.C. and the dispersion of the Jews after the destruction of the temple in 70 A.D.

A second concern is that the four Gospels are not in complete harmony. These critics note that each Gospel covers different aspects of Christ's life, with certain observations made by only one or two of the four authors. But that concern can be dispelled by understanding that the four Gospels were written by *different* authors, addressed to *different* audiences. Today, as always, we communicate differently to children than to adults, to the very educated versus the uneducated, to those with similar backgrounds as opposed to those with no shared experiences. Even locality, financial standing, and personal interests can change the way our audience understands us.

Because we communicate to be understood, we naturally adjust our message to match our audience.

Matthew directed his testimony to the Jews. Mark, to the Romans and the Gentiles. Luke, a physician, wrote primarily for the benefit of the Greeks and others of culture and refinement. John testified mainly to the believers, those already referred to as saints. And in addition to having different audiences, the four writers had very different backgrounds, which would obviously affect their perspectives, interests, and writing styles.

Matthew

Matthew was a member of Christ's original assembly called the Quorum of the Twelve Apostles. He was a publican, or tax collector, before Christ called him to come and follow. His job indicates he probably had more education than some of his fellow apostles, since he would have needed skills in reading, writing, and arithmetic to collect taxes. Throughout Christ's ministry he may have taken notes recording Christ's teachings and activities. He may have drawn upon them and his own recollections while writing his Gospel message for the Hebrews—in their own dialect.

Mark

Mark was not a member of Christ's original company of twelve. He grew up in Jerusalem and is most certainly the same Mark whose mother's home served as the meeting place in Jerusalem for the early disciples. He was a young man when Jesus came to the upper room for the Last Supper. It is believed that Mark, at the arrest of Christ at the Garden of Gethsemane, was the ". . . certain young man, having a linen cloth cast about his naked body; and the young men laid hold on him: and he left the linen cloth, and fled from them naked" (Mark 14:51–52). Mark is the only Gospel writer who shares this detail.

Mark is said to have accompanied Paul and Barnabas on their missionary journey to Cyprus. On another occasion he served the apostle Peter as an interpreter. Of the four Gospel testimonies, his was believed to be the first written, and it accurately portrays the different groups in Jewish Palestine at the time of Christ.

Luke

Luke was a close associate of the early apostles. Paul refers to him as "Luke, the beloved physician . . . " (Colossians 4:14). His background explains his special interest in the virgin birth, being the only one of the four Gospel writers to mention it. Also, as a physician he was in a unique position to investigate the many healings that Christ performed, including the greatest healing—Christ's own resurrection. Luke became a companion to the apostle Paul. His writings reveal a passion for accurate detail.

John

John the Beloved, one of the original twelve apostles, is the writer of the fourth Gospel, which was addressed to the disciples of Christ. John's testimony was intended to guide Christ's believers to a more complete and profound understanding of the Master's life and mission. John knew that his work would be incomplete, conveying only a small portion of what he knew and saw of Christ's life. He writes, "And there are also many other things which Jesus did, the which, if they should be written every one, I suppose even the world itself could not contain the books that should be written. Amen" (John 21:25).

Scholars have universally acclaimed the King James version of the Bible as containing some of the most forceful, direct, and majestic prose ever applied in the English language. Since the King James version is readily available and is concise and descriptive in the Gospel narratives, the author has chosen it for all Bible references in this volume.

As a final thought to the reader, because the trial of Christ is a most sacred subject, if it is approached prayerfully, the message within these pages can yield powerful new personal insights into the life—and death—of our Lord and Savior Jesus Christ.

TWO

THIS IS BLASPHEMY

Matthew 26:65 ". . . behold now ye have heard his blasphemy"

Neither the Old nor the New Testament contains a physical description of our Lord Jesus Christ. In spite of the absence of such a description, many talented artists have succeeded in capturing on canvas a certain gentleness or goodness or heavenly quality that has helped us picture the Savior for ourselves. Perhaps reading this book can enhance your mental image of Christ. Perhaps you can learn to know a little better and love a little more the physical man Jesus. The human side. And perhaps, as the last few days of his life unfold before you, so will the divinity of his mission.

Before Christ began his ministry, two major events had taken place: he had been baptized by John the Baptist,[1] and he had been led by the spirit into the wilderness, where he fasted for forty days and endured the temptations of Satan.[2] At this point, Christ knew who he was and understood that he was now to embark upon his life's work.

Jesus performed his first miracle at a wedding feast in Cana by turning water into fine wine.[3] He subsequently returned to his home town of Nazareth. When he entered the synagogue on the Sabbath day, he was approached by the leader of the holy house. This leader invited him to be the Sheliach Tishbur, or the delegate of the congregation. This meant Christ was to read from the Law and the Prophets and to then expound upon his reading. To be asked thus was a distinct honor that was bestowed only upon a person of dignity, humility, modesty, and a knowledge of the scriptures. This honor was usually reserved for some great Rabbi, famed preacher, or distinguished person with whom the congregation was familiar. It was understood that the chosen Sheliach Tishbur had a thorough understanding of the scriptures.[4]

When a person was appointed as the delegate for the congregation, it was the custom for him to ascend to the lectern where the minister would hand him the selected passage from

---

[1] Matthew 3:13, 16–17; Mark 1:9–11; Luke 3:21–22; John 1:29–32

[2] Matthew 4:1–11; Mark 1:13; Luke 4:1–13

[3] John 2:1–12

[4] For a more complete review of preaching in the synagogue, see Alfred Edersheim, *The Life and Times of Jesus the Messiah* (Grand Rapids, Michigan: Wm. B. Eerdmans Publishing Co., 1971) 430–459.

the Law and the Prophets. The Sheliach Tishbur would read the passage while standing at the lectern. Then he would be seated and expound upon what he had just read.

In this instance, the minister had ". . . delivered unto him the book of the prophet Esaias. And when he had opened the book, he found the place where it was written, The Spirit of the Lord is upon me, because he hath anointed me to preach the gospel to the poor; he hath sent me to heal the broken hearted, to preach deliverance to the captives, and recovering of sight to the blind, to set at liberty them that are bruised, to preach the acceptable year of the Lord. And he closed the book, and he gave it again to the minister, and sat down. And the eyes of all them that were in the synagogue were fastened on him" (Luke 4:17–20).

It is no wonder the eyes were fastened upon him. The scripture that Christ had read was of great interest to all Jews, referring to the Messiah who was to come. But perhaps more interesting than the subject of the text was the reader of the words. Since the wedding feast had taken place only four miles away, it is probable that the miracle of Christ's turning water to wine had become common knowledge in the city of Nazareth. There would have been a high interest among the congregation to hear from this man who had performed the miracle and was from their own town.

But it is almost certain that no one in the audience expected to hear the words that Jesus uttered: ". . . This day is this scripture fulfilled in your ears" (Luke 4:21).

They were astounded and asked among themselves, ". . . Is not this Joseph's son?" (Luke 4:22) This man who had grown up in their community, who had shared their lives, was now claiming to fulfill the prophecy of the prophet Isaiah to be the Messiah. That was blasphemy!

Then Jesus expounded further. "And all they in the synagogue, when they heard these things, were filled with wrath, And rose up, and thrust him out of the city, and led him unto the brow of the hill whereon their city was built, that they might cast him down headlong [to stone him without so much as a trial]. But he passing through the midst of them went his way . . ." (Luke 4:28–30).

From that moment, Jesus was a marked man. Marked by the leaders of the synagogue and by the leaders of the Sanhedrin—who were the leaders of the Jewish nation.

Other activities that made Jesus a marked man include the cleansing of the temple. Near both the beginning and end of his ministry Christ took it upon himself to cleanse the temple at Jerusalem. The temple was not just a religious symbol to the Jews, it signified their power and authority. At the time of Passover, thousands would come from all over the country. Visitors would bring the currency from their own nation. Such foreign currencies were not accepted in the temple for the purchase of the sacrificial animals. So the House of Hanan (the leaders of the Sanhedrin) set up booths for money exchange in the courts of the temple. Those who exchanged currency would make a profit in the exchange. The patron would have to purchase an animal for a temple offering and, in addition, pay an annual temple tax. That brought further revenue into the temple coffers.

Jesus condemned these actions. Such doings made His house and His Father's house a house of commerce. He said to the religious leaders, "make not my Father's house an house of merchandise" (John 2:16). With that he poured out the changer's money, drove the changers out of the temple, over-turned the tables, and drove out the animals.

About three years later, after his second cleansing of the temple, Christ stood on the Mount of Olives, looked over the temple mount and exclaimed "O Jerusalem, . . . how often would I have gathered thy children together, even as a hen gathereth her chickens under her wings, and ye would not! Behold your house (notice he did not say His Father's house, but *your* house) is left unto you desolate" (Matthew 23:37–38). By those words Jesus rejected the temple as His Father's house.

The apostle John narrates three additional episodes unique to his gospel that explain why the Jews demanded Jesus' death.

The first episode is the healing of an invalid on the Sabbath. Early in his ministry, Jesus would go to Jerusalem for one of the feasts. There by a pool lay a number of infirm people with var-ious maladies. There was a superstition that each year an angel would come down and would touch the waters. The belief was that the first person who got into the pool would be cured of his or her malady. One man who was an invalid for 38 years went to the pool every year. Because of his condition, he was unable to be the first one to get into the pool. Jesus saw him and said, "wilt thou be made whole? The impotent man answered him, Sir, I have no man when the water is troubled to put me into the pool." Jesus said unto him, "rise, take up thy bed and walk" (John 5:6–8) and immediately the man was healed and he picked up his bed and he walked down the street. The problem was, it was on the Sabbath. Carrying his bed, he had violated Jewish law. The local Jewish leaders asked the man who had healed him and he answered it was Jesus. John then reports: "And therefore did the Jews persecute Jesus, and sought to slay him, because he had done these things on the sabbath day. But Jesus answered them, My Father worketh hitherto, and I work. Therefore the Jews sought the more to kill him, because he not only had broken the sabbath, but said also that God was his Father, making himself equal with God" (John 5:16–18).

Remember that accusation; it will be cited later when the Jews accuse Jesus of blasphemy. Can you see how John ascribes to the Jewish leadership a motive for their desire to kill Jesus? He had made himself a God.

The second episode is the feeding of the five thousand. This episode marked the high point of Jesus' ministry. Having compassion on this large crowd that followed him, Jesus miraculously multiplied five loaves and two small fishes and fed the entire multitude. The miracle became the basis for one of his most remarkable sermons. The day following the miracle, the multitude came searching for Jesus. On this occasion he boldly announced to them that it was he who gave manna to the Israelites in their sojourn to the promised land. He was the promised Messiah. "I am the living bread which came down from heaven: if any man eat of this bread, he shall live for ever: and the bread that I will give is my flesh, which I will give for the life of the world" (John 6:51).

That was a startling declaration to those people. The pronouncement "I Am" in their language was regarded as blasphemy. "I Am" meant "I am Jehovah. The God of Abraham, Isaac, and Jacob." John tells of another episode where Jesus announced to the Jews "before Abraham was, I am" (John 8:58). For that bold announcement they sought his life.

Jesus ministered among the Jews for about two and one-half years, principally in Galilee. Many had heard his teachings and some had accepted the fact that he was the promised Messiah. He was at the height of his popularity and now he took occasion to separate the true believers from the weak.

In the context of his discourse on the bread of life Jesus said, "Whoso eateth my flesh, and drinketh my blood, hath eternal life; and I will raise him up at the last day" (John 6:54). That expression obviously referred to his later introduction of the sacrament. But it also referred to accepting him as the living bread and water, the promised Messiah, the Son of God . . . and then abiding by his doctrine. That was hard doctrine and it had a serious effect on the disciples who professed to follow after him.

"Many therefore of his disciples, when they heard this, said, This is an hard saying" (John 6:60). Then John adds this sad commentary: "From that time many of his disciples went back, and walked no more with him" (John 6:66). This hard doctrine sifted the wheat from the chaff.

The third episode recorded by John is the raising of Lazarus. All four gospel writers tell of this miracle but only John's record clearly tells us about the conspiracy among the Jewish leaders to kill Jesus. The miracle of raising Lazarus from the dead is sometimes referred to as the irrefutable miracle. It was irrefutable for three reasons.

First, it was intentionally done in public so that no one could challenge the fact that a miracle occurred. Second, it discredited the superstition that the spirit hovered over the body for only three days and then left forever. Jesus waited four days before he came to the tomb of Lazarus and then called him forth on the fourth day. Third, he desired to leave an irrefutable witness that he was the Son of God, the resurrection and the life so that His nation and His disciples would have all the proof necessary that he indeed was the Son of God.

It was in the context of this miracle that Jesus said to Martha, "I am the resurrection and the life: he that believeth in me, though he were dead, yet shall he live" (John 11:25). The miracle had two outcomes. Jews who witnessed the miracle believed on him. But others, unbelieving, went and told the Pharisees about the miracle. The miracle caused such alarm among the Jewish leaders that they convened a council to decide the question "What do we? for this man doeth many miracles" (John 11:47). John then tells us of the motive that they had for the conspiracy to kill Jesus.

"If we let him thus alone, all men will believe on him: and the Romans shall come and take away both our place and our nation" (John 11:48). Jesus had to be destroyed if they were to retain the limited authority which the Romans had granted to them. It was at this point Caiaphus the high priest prophesied that Jesus would die for the nation (John 11:51). John then adds this postscript for this episode: "Then from that day forth they took counsel together for to put him to death" (John 11:53).

And so begins our journey through the illegal trials of Christ.

THREE

ROMAN RULERS AROUND THE TIME OF CHRIST

Luke 3:1 "Now in the fifteenth year of the reign
of Tiberius Caesar. . ."

No period of history is more important than the few years when Jesus Christ walked the earth. His three short years of ministry hold the answers to virtually all the problems of life. His last few days of mortality satisfy the very demands of justice, enabling man to divest himself of sin and return to his God and Creator.

Understanding the political and legal climate surrounding Christ's life is key to appreciating the mockery of justice he endured during his last week of mortal ministry those 2,000 years ago. Becoming better acquainted with the people involved in history at the time of Christ's life and what the rules were, leads to a better comprehension of what really happened and why. The lives of these people often come across as vividly as characters in a modern day television soap opera. Try to catch a feeling for what are the rules and who are the players in this drama. To begin this review may seem a little tedious to the reader. Stick with it. You'll be glad you did. Little details will begin to jump out at you from the story, which you might have otherwise missed.

The First Four Rulers of the Roman Empire to Have Jurisdiction Over Palestine

Pompey the Great served as Imperator[5] of Rome from about 81 to 48 B.C., invading and conquering Palestine in 63 B.C. and beginning Rome's 700-year rule over the area. Thus, Palestine became a "client state,"[6] ruled by a Roman procurator.[7]

At the death of Pompey, Julius Caesar assumed the title of dictator, ruling the Roman Republic until his assassination on March 15, 44 B.C. In Caesar's will, he ordered a post-mortum adoption of his grandnephew Gaius Octavius (who later became known as Augustus Caesar), designating him his heir.

On August 19, 44 B.C., three months after Julius Caesar's death, 19-year-old Octavius was elected consul of Rome and

---

[5] *Imperator:* Not officially an emperor, but a strong general who amassed enough power to take over actual control of the government—even though the Senate was officially responsible for governing Rome and her conquered provinces.

[6] *Client state:* A nation dependent on another politically, economically, etc.

[7] *Procurator:* An official of ancient Rome who managed the financial affairs of a province or acted as governor of a lesser province. A procurator was considered a personal representative—a political substitute—of Caesar.

formally adopted as the son of Caesar. A year later he began his rule as part of the Second Triumvirate,[8] governing Rome along-side Lepidus and Mark Anthony of Cleopatra fame. Within 15 years of Julius Caesar's death, Octavius became the first emperor to the Republic, ruling from approximately 31 B.C. to A.D. 14., including the early years of Christ's life. Although his leadership of Rome was designated by his predecessor and supported by the army, the Roman Senate went through the motions of electing him officially. In 27 B.C., the Senate gave him the title Augustus, meaning "revered" or "venerated." He did much to improve the temporal affairs of his empire—building roads, aqueducts, and numerous buildings while establishing his empire through personal control.

In family life, Augustus was less successful. He had only one child of his own, a daughter, Julia—known for flaunting her lewd and coarse conduct, including adultery. Hoping to arrange an heir through Julia, Augustus forced Marcellus to marry her. After the death of Marcellus, Marcus Agrippa was chosen to be her second husband. Julia had two sons, Caius and Lucius, by Agrippa before he died. But this did not satisfy Augustus. He wanted Julia to marry his stepson, Tiberius, the son of his wife Livia.[9] Augustus wanted an heir from this union.

At this time Tiberius was married to Vispania. Even though Tiberius loved his wife, Vispania, Augustus compelled him to divorce her. He was to marry Augustus' daughter, Julia, in

---

[8] *Triumvirate:* Government by three persons or by a coalition of three parties.

[9] *Livia:* When Augustus Caesar needed the political connections of Livia's family, he arranged for her to be divorced from her first husband. Augustus married Livia when Tiberius was about three years old.

order to be in line for power. But when Julia and Tiberius (he was actually Julia's stepbrother!) were married, they were extremely unhappy. Their characters were so different, they didn't make a happy couple. Eventually Tiberius—who had wept at seeing his beloved ex-wife Vispania remarry—left Julia and went to live on the Island of Rhodes. Julia's debaucheries became so notorious that Augustus was compelled to banish her from Rome; she was never allowed to return. While she was banished, Julia had an illicit affair with a Roman soldier and gave birth to a daughter named Claudia.

By A.D. 4, both grandsons, Caius and Lucius, who were the only heirs of Augustus, had died. Caius was ambushed by his enemies and died while trying to return home. Lucius died suddenly on his way to Spain. It was rumored that the cause of his death was poison provided by his step-mother, Livia, who wanted to clear the way for Tiberius to become Emperor.

Two years later, Augustus appointed his stepson Tiberius (who later became Tiberius Caesar) to become his heir and successor. Tiberius, a soldier by training, was pursuing a battle campaign in a distant part of the empire when he was summoned to Rome. Augustus, now 76 years of age, was taken gravely ill. Tiberius was at his bedside just in time to hear Augustus breathe his last sigh. He died on August 19 in 14 A.D. It was said that what killed Augustus was neither old age nor illness. It was suspected that his wife Livia poisoned some figs on the branch of the tree from which the old Emperor enjoyed picking and eating while walking through the garden.

After a show of reluctance, Tiberius allowed the Roman Senate to proclaim him Emperor. Tiberius ruled Rome for 23 years—from A.D. 14 to his own death in A.D. 37. He was ruler of the Roman Empire during the trials of Christ.

Tiberius had some good qualities. He was a capable administrator who carefully supervised tax collection and spending, and selected efficient governors to rule throughout the Empire. Despite his capabilities, he had some deficiencies of character. He was paranoid about retaining his hard-to-come-by position and he was suspicious of the Senate. To assure and secure his position he had at least 52 men put to death (including his probable successor) whom he suspected of conspiring to take over the Empire.

These four leaders—Pompey the Great, Julius Caesar, Augustus Caesar, and Tiberius Caesar—were the first to rule over Palestine as part of the Roman Empire. Although Augustus and Tiberius reigned during the life of Christ, they took little interest in distant Palestine. Instead of managing it in person, they appointed governors, or procurators, to rule in their place.

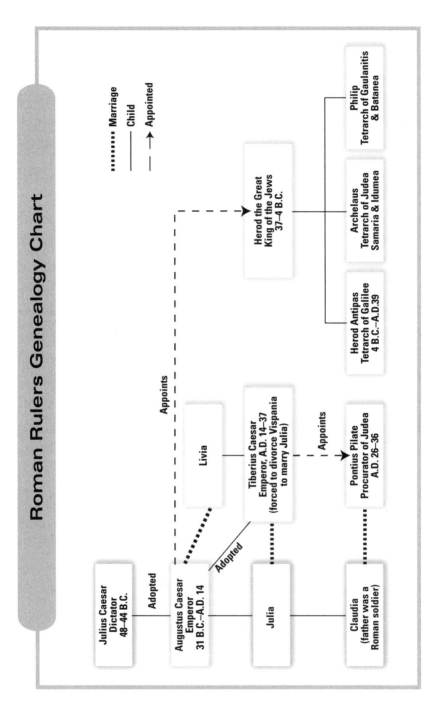

Roman Rulers Genealogy Chart

Pontius Pilate—Roman Procurator Over Judea

Pontius Pilate was the fifth Roman procurator of Judea, serving from A.D. 26 to 36. As procurator during those years, he allowed the execution of Jesus of Nazareth. An understanding of Pilate's background helps clarify his role in that pivotal event.

Little is known of Pilate's early life. He was born in Seville, Spain, but switched allegiance to the Romans after they conquered his mother country. Seeking his fortune in Rome, Pilate married 15-year-old Claudia, the youngest daughter of Julia. (Remember now, Julia was Augustus Caesar's only child and she was the second wife of Tiberius Caesar.) Because Claudia was the granddaughter of Augustus Caesar, Pilate hoped his marriage to her would result in an imperial appointment. This ambition was fulfilled when, as a wedding gift, Tiberius presented him with a commission as procurator of Judea.

Pilate's new commission probably left him somewhat disappointed, since Judea was not a prestigious appointment. It was simply a way for Tiberius to remove Pilate and Claudia as far from Rome as possible, because he was not overly fond of them. If you look at a map, you will see that in the Roman Empire Judea was about as far away from Rome as any area in the Empire.

Although not prestigious, filling the role of procurator of Judea was no easy task. Prior to Pilate, Roman procurators had been careful not to offend the Jews. This courtesy included avoiding any public display of Roman flags and emblems. When Pilate took office, he lacked the political savvy to continue that practice of discretion. He was *not* careful to accommodate the Jews. He entered Jerusalem with standards emblazoned with the images of the Emperor Tiberius, making his job as procurator more difficult than it had been for his predecessors.

Pilate's arrogance offended and infuriated the Jews. Their second commandment dictated against worldly images, and they were wroth to witness Pilate's flagrant display of contempt for their Holy City. For five days they petitioned him to remove the offensive standards, but he refused to hear their arguments, let alone consider them. When Pilate finally admitted the Jews to the judgment seat to be officially heard, he ordered his soldiers to surround them, and then he threatened them with instant death if they did not stop bothering him over the matter. The citizens of Jerusalem called his bluff. In open defiance, the outraged Jews threw themselves to the ground and bared their necks for the Roman swords, preferring to die rather than submit to the violation of their sacred laws. Outmaneuvered and outclassed—and not willing to kill so many—Pilate yielded and withdrew the standards. This political blunder at the beginning of his appointment highlighted his lack of talent and discretion. This one act embarrassed him and had a residual influence on all the actions of his subsequent career.

Having learned little, Pilate later appropriated funds from the temple treasury and used them to complete an aqueduct that was to bring water to Jerusalem. Because the Jews reverenced the *corban*, or temple money, they were highly offended that their sacred funds had been used for this worldly purpose. Once again, Pilate faced a crowd of Jews, gathered in clamor against him.

But this time Pilate did not ignore them for days or threaten their death. Instead, he ordered soldiers to disguise themselves as Jews and mingle with the crowd. On his signal, the soldiers attacked the unarmed Jews, beating them severely and quelling the riot. As one might expect, hatred for Pilate grew and festered in the hearts of his subjects.

In a further attempt to establish his authority, Pilate later adorned his palace with gilded shields dedicated to the Emperor Tiberius. Outraged, the Jewish leaders circumvented their enemy-leader, petitioning directly to Tiberius, stating that the shields were hung less for his honor than for the annoyance of the Jewish people. Tiberius granted their request, ordering the removal of the shields from the palace in Jerusalem. Pilate had these images transferred to the temple of Augustus at Caesarea.

As procurator, Pilate was to act as an extension of Tiberius and did not want to displease him. He understood Tiberius' tendency toward paranoia and knew he had to be somewhat careful, even that far from Rome. However, Pilate's actions show his inability to plan beyond the scope of his own meager pride, a disabling weakness that kept him from adequately representing Tiberius. In contrast with his strategic and powerful emperor, Pilate was wicked and self-absorbed. He appeared to spurn his subjects, the Jews, rather than to govern them efficiently. He may have retained a distaste for his appointment because of being sent so far away from the real seat of power—Rome.

Herod the Great—Jewish King Over Judea

Another player in our cast of characters is Herod, pro-claimed King of the Jews in 37 B.C. by Augustus Caesar. This prestige was awarded because of Herod's support for the Romans and because Herod's father, Antipater—an Arab Sheikh from southern Palestine—had at one time come to the military aid of Augustus Caesar. Apparently not satisfied with the title of *king*, he dubbed himself *Herod the Great*.

Even though Judea was a conquered nation, the Jews were allowed to govern themselves internally to some degree. By his marriage to Mariamne, the daughter of Simon Maccabee, a high priest, Herod the Great allied himself with the family of the Maccabees. This family had led the patriotic party of the Jews for several generations. As a convert to Judaism, Herod had power not only as an appointee of Rome, but also as a Jewish citizen.

In about 20 B.C. King Herod the Great began rebuilding the temple in Jerusalem.[10] In spite of this obvious tribute to the Jews, they hated him. And justly so, for many reasons. First, Herod the Great had ordered the heartless murdering of ". . . all the chil-dren that were in Bethlehem, and in all the coasts thereof, from two years old and under . . . " (Matthew 2:16) at the time of the birth of Christ. Also, in violation of Jewish law, he had taken

---

[10] *The temple at Jerusalem:* "Founded by King Solomon in the tenth century B.C., destroyed by the armies of Babylon in 587 B.C., and rebuilt by the Jews who returned to Jerusalem after the captivity. A few years before the birth of Christ, King Herod began replacing it with a new, larger temple, commonly called the Second Temple. This magnificent structure took many years to build, and it was barely completed by 70 A.D. when it was demolished by the Romans." John Michell, *The Temple at Jerusalem: A Revelation* (Boston: Weiser Books, 2001) 1.

unto himself ten wives. Finally, in a fit of jealousy, he had murdered seven members of his own family, including three sons, one wife, and her mother. Herod the Great's murderous fame was not limited to Judea. While signing a third death warrant for one of Herod's sons, Augustus Caesar remarked that he would rather be a pig in Herod's court than be Herod's son!

At Herod's death, and with the consent of Rome, Herod's will divided his kingdom among his three surviving sons:

1. To his son Archelaus—Judea, Samaria and Idumea
2. To his son Phillip—Gaulanitis and Batanea
3. To his son Herod Antipas—Galilee and Perea

Herod Antipas—Tetrarch Over Galilee

Herod Antipas received the title "Tetrarch[11] of Galilee" from his father's will. When his brother Archelaus died, Herod Antipas believed that his dead brother's kingdom, which included Judea, should be consolidated with his own. Instead, the rule of Judea was given to Pontius Pilate. This may have caused the animosity that existed between Pilate and Herod Antipas. Later you will learn that they were made friends again after Pilate sends Christ to Herod for interrogation at his palace in Jerusalem.

Though Herod Antipas was not the insane, murdering monster his father had been, history records his many faults—he was a perpetual drunkard and morally corrupt. He was so depraved that he beheaded John the Baptist, who was innocent of any crime. The Pharisees warned Christ that Herod Antipas would kill him also.

---

[11] *Tetrarch:* In the ancient Roman Empire, the ruler of part of a province.

Summary of Roman Rulers

Dates	Name	Birth–Death
Rulers over Rome		
About 81–48 B.C.	Pompey the Great	About 106–48 B.C.
48–44 B.C.	Julius Caesar	100–44 B.C.
31 B.C.–A.D. 14	Gaius Octavius (Augustus Caesar)	63 B.C.–A.D. 14
A.D. 14–37	Tiberius Claudius Nero (Tiberius Caesar)	42 B.C.–A.D. 37
Rulers over Palestine		
A.D. 26–36	Pontius Pilate (Procurator of Judea)	Birth–death unknown
37–4 B.C.	Herod the Great (King of the Jews)	73–4 B.C. to 1 B.C.[12]
4 B.C.–A.D. 39	Herod Antipas (Tetrarch of Galilee)	Unknown–A.D. 40

---

[12] "The primary source of the life of Herod is the book written by Josephus, a Jewish historian. His methods are not always clear, and his results are sometimes inconsistent. Usually the strongest evidence to correlate history with our calendar is to compare events which are also dated in Roman history. Josephus mentions a lunar eclipse shortly before the death of King Herod. The date of this lunar eclipse has long been recognized as an important date in determining possible dates for the birth of Christ. For many years it has been considered that the eclipse may have occurred on what we would now call March 13, 4 B.C. Because of this, Christ must have been born about 6 - 5 B.C. However, recent study has raised questions about that eclipse and now two other dates are considered to be preferred. One occurring on January 10, 1 B.C. and one which occurred on December 29, 1 B.C. This date would suggest that Christ was born during the Passover season of 1 B.C. If that date is selected, it is probable that Herod died in 1 A.D. after the birth of Christ and after causing the death of children in Bethlehem and all the coasts thereof. Other facts and events seem to support this conclusion." John P. Pratt, "Yet Another Eclipse for Herod," *The Planetarian,* Vol 19, No. 4 December 1990: 8–14.

FOUR

HEBREW LEADERSHIP— THE SANHEDRIN

Mark 10:33 ". . . and the Son of Man shall be delivered unto the chief priests . . ."

Early in Hebrew history, becoming a member of the Great Sanhedrin was the highest honor a man could achieve; the Sanhedrin[13] held supreme authority in all matters, both secular and religious. When the Jews were conquered by Rome they were still allowed to govern themselves as long as they didn't interfere with Roman law. The Jewish nation was a client state; Roman law was supreme. But when Roman governors began appointing and removing members of the Sanhedrin, this governing body became corrupt.

---

[13] *Sanhedrin* denotes a legislative assembly or ecclesiastical council which deliberates in a sitting posture.

Around the time of Christ, the Jewish court system was led by a corrupt Sanhedrin that administered (alleged) justice in Palestine according to the Mosaic law. The Great Sanhedrin, with 71 members, was the supreme religious body in Palestine. Outlying larger cities also had their own local governing body known as the Lesser Sanhedrin, composed of 23 members.

There were also Lower Tribunals in smaller towns or villages, which consisted of three temporary judges who would briefly fill the position in order to rule on a crime. One judge would be selected by the accuser; a second, by the accused; and a third, by the first two judges.

Similar to the United States judicial system, the lower tribunal functioned much like our cities' Justice of the Peace Courts; the Lesser Sanhedrin, similar to our counties' Superior Courts; and the Great Sanhedrin, analogous to our nation's Supreme Court.

The Great Sanhedrin was patterned after the council of the 70 that Moses had established some 1,500 years earlier. Its 71 members were divided into three chambers, or quorums, each consisting of 23 men. The chamber of priests was filled exclusively by those who held the rank of high priest. The chamber of scribes included Levites, doctors, and laymen who were especially familiar with the law. The chamber of the ancients (or elders) was comprised of the most elderly and respected men of the nation. In addition, there was one *chief high priest* who served as president of the whole council, and one *father of the tribunal* who operated in a similar position to our vice-president. To conduct a tribunal, or court, at least one quorum was required, at least 23 of the 71 members had to be present. At the time of Christ, the Great Sanhedrin was comprised of approximately 80 percent Sadducees[14] and 20 percent Pharisees[15] and Herodians.[16]

The Great Sanhedrin met daily in the Chamber of Hewn Stones, a room on the temple grounds. They determined if any violations of Jewish law had taken place in Jewish communities. If someone were found guilty, the Great Sanhedrin decided the appropriate punishment. At one time, they could order people to be whipped, scourged, or put to death. However, at the time of Christ the Great Sanhedrin did not have power to sentence a person to death without the consent of Rome. Only King Herod or a Roman procurator could sentence a person to die.

Membership in the Sanhedrin was open to men only, and every member had to meet specific requirements:

1. He must be a lineal descendant of Hebrew parents.
2. He must be learned in the law, both written and oral.
3. He must have judicial experience.
4. He must be learned in the sciences—especially well-grounded in astronomy, medicine, and chemistry.

---

[14] *Sadducee:* A member of an ancient, aristocratic Jewish party, representing the ruling hierarchy that accepted only the written Mosaic law and rejected the oral or traditional law; Sadducees were the majority party in the Sanhedrin. They taught of a free will in morals—immorality. They didn't believe in the resurrection. Opposed to Pharisee.

[15] *Pharisee:* A member of an ancient Jewish sect that emphasized strict interpretation and careful observance of the Mosaic law in both its written and oral (or traditional) form; they did believe in the resurrection. Opposed to Sadducee.

[16] *Herodian:* One of a party among the Jews, composed of partisans of Herod of Galilee. They joined with the Pharisees against Christ.

5. He must be an accomplished linguist, thoroughly familiar with the languages of the surrounding nations.
   (Interpreters were not allowed in Hebrew courts.)
6. He must be modest, popular, of good appearance, and
   free from haughtiness. (By the time a judge had worked
   his way through the lower courts, it was expected that
   he would naturally possess these virtues.)
7. He must be pious, strong, and courageous—showing
   that his judgments will be just and righteous.
8. He must be the father of a family.
9. He must be at least 40 years of age.

Disqualification from membership in the Great Sanhedrin
was also amazingly specific:

1. A man who had never had any regular trade, occupa-
   tion, or profession by which he gained his livelihood
   was disqualified.
2. Gamblers, dice players, bettors on pigeon matches,
   usurers, and slave dealers were disqualified. (These
   activities were regarded as forms of thievery—and
   thieves were not eligible to sit as judges.)
3. A man who had dealt in the fruits of the seventh year[17]
   was disqualified. (Under the law of Moses, every seventh year the land was to rest, with nothing planted,
   cultivated, or pruned. A person who dealt in the fruits
   of the seventh year was deemed lacking in conscience.)

---

[17] *Seventh year:* "But in the seventh year shall be a sabbath of rest unto the
land, a sabbath for the Lord: thou shalt neither sow thy field, nor prune thy
vineyard" (Leviticus 25:4).

4. The King could not be a member of the Great Sanhedrin.

In addition, the following conditions could disqualify a Sanhedrin member from participation in a specific trial:

1. In trials where the death penalty might be inflicted, an aged man or an illegitimate son was disqualified.
2. A man who was concerned with or interested in a matter to be adjudicated was disqualified. (If one were personally interested in a matter, impartiality might be impossible.)
3. Any relative of the accused, of whatever degree, was disqualified.
4. A person who would become an heir, or might otherwise benefit from the outcome of the trial or death of the accused, was disqualified.

Becoming a member of the Great Sanhedrin required rigorous screening, but offered a great degree of respect and power. The chief judge of the Great Sanhedrin was also the chief high priest of Israel, making him the most powerful Jewish leader.

Annas was the chief high priest of Israel from A.D. 7–15, meaning he was probably the chief high priest when the young Christ taught the priests in the temple. Annas was wicked and adulterous, a corrupt leader. At one time, he carried out a death sentence without the proper approval of the Roman authorities and was removed from office by Rome. Even though he lost his official title, Annas still exercised his authority in the Great Sanhedrin through members of his family. In the years after he was removed from office, five of his sons, his son-in-law Caiaphas, and his grandson Matthias, also became high priests.

Even after Annas had been officially released as chief high priest and another was legally named in his stead, many of the stricter Jews still looked to Annas as *God's* high priest.

At the time of the trial of Christ, the House of Hanan was the most influential family in the Jewish nation, and Annas, whose true Jewish name was Hanan, the younger, was the patriarch of that family. The House of Hanan operated the store that was referred to as "the four shops under the twin cedars of olivet," which sold the legally pure sacrificial animals at the temple. Because he controlled the temple traffic, Annas was probably one of the richest men in Israel.

Caiaphas, the son-in-law of Annas, was the chief high priest during the trials of Christ. That he wanted Jesus put to death is not surprising, since, among other things, Jesus decried the money changing at the temple. If Christ's teachings were accepted, Annas and Caiaphas would lose the great profits they made by selling sacrificial animals in that sacred edifice.

FIVE

HEBREW LAW

Joshua 8:31 ". . . as it is written in the book
of the law of Moses . . ."

Hebrew law followed strict rules of procedure. The accused Jesus was unlawfully condemned during his trial because many of these rules were broken.[18] As you read through these Hebrew Rules of Procedure, see if you can identify which ones were broken.

---

[18] A most interesting and more complete discussion of the Hebrew Rules of Procedure, Evidence and Witnesses, is found in Walter M. Chandler, *The Trial of Jesus* (New York: The Empire Publishing Co., 1908) also Edersheim, *The Life and Times of Jesus the Messiah.*

Rules of Procedure

1. Proceedings were to be held during the day; no process was allowed to begin at night.

2. Proceedings could begin only *after* the morning sacrifice at the temple.

3. Proceedings were to be held *only* in the Chamber of Hewn Stones (a temple chamber).

4. In the Chamber, the seating was arranged in a semi-circle, with the accused facing the judges.

5. At least 23 members of the Great Sanhedrin were required to form a quorum that would try a case.

6. Two writers were present to take down any testimony, including speeches by the judges, spoken in favor of, or against, the accused.

7. Prejudiced judges could not participate in the trial.

8. No proceedings could be held on Sabbaths **or** feast days or on the *eves* of Sabbaths or feast days. (The eves of Sabbaths and feast days were not considered sacred. But a trial held on the eves of those days could create a problem. If a death sentence was pronounced, the law required that a second trial be held the following day. As the following day would be a Sabbath or feast day—days that *were* considered sacred—a second trial would be a violation of Jewish law.)

9. Sanhedrin members could not originate charges, nor could they witness against the accused.

10. Hebrew Rules of Witnesses and Evidence had to be maintained. (These rules immediately follow the Rules of Procedure.)

11. The merits of a defense had to be heard.

12. No rending of clothes was allowed. (If the chief priest rent his clothes, that signified that he felt the defendant was guilty of a grievous sin, and serious action needed to be taken against that defendant. Obviously, such a display would seriously prejudice any decision related to that case.)

13. A vote determined the verdict. Seated around the table or room in order of seniority, beginning with the most recently appointed, members voted on the charges.

14. A unanimous verdict of guilty had the same effect as an acquittal. (If the vote were unanimous against the defendant, the judges were deemed prejudiced against him, as if the defendant's fate had been predetermined.)

15. If a death sentence were pronounced, a second trial was to be held the following day.

16. If two trials were needed, the judges had to fast and pray between them.

17. On the second day of trial, a judge could change his vote only from guilty to not guilty.

Rules of Witnesses and Evidence

The Hebrews had exact rules for many aspects of their lives, especially involving the governing of people. Following are the Hebrew Rules of Witnesses and Evidence. They are particularly important as they apply to the trial of Christ.

1. **Competency:** Under Hebrew law, the qualifications of a competent witness were almost identical to those of

a qualified judge; all persons not incompetent were, by default, competent.

2. **Incompetency:** The following persons were considered incompetent as witnesses: Gentiles, minors, slaves, idiots and lunatics, deaf mutes, blind men, gamblers, usurers, illiterate or immodest persons, persons who had been convicted of irreligion or immorality, relatives, publicans (tax gathers), and all persons directly interested in the case. Women were also considered incompetent, but not because the Sanhedrin didn't trust the testimony of a woman. According to Jewish law, the death sentence was carried out by the witnesses against the accused, so the women were not allowed to witness because the Sanhedrin didn't want their women to have to carry out a death sentence to those found guilty.

3. **Number required to convict:** Under Hebrew law, three eyewitnesses, including the prosecuting witness, were required for a conviction.

4. **No oath required:** An oath, in the modern sense, was never administered.

5. **Prior examination of witnesses:** To prevent the admission of irrelevant or illegal testimony, a special committee of the Sanhedrin conducted a private, preliminary examination of the witnesses. All irrelevant testimony divulged at this private examination was declared inadmissible and was cast aside.

6. **Agreement of witnesses:** The witnesses were required to agree on all essential details. If not, their testimonies were rejected as invalid.

7. **Separation of witnesses:** The witnesses were required to give their testimony separately, in the presence of the accused, but not in the presence of other witnesses.

8. **Mode of examination of witnesses:** The examination of witnesses included two distinct sets of questions. The first set related to the time and place of the alleged crime. These questions were prescribed by law and could not vary. The second set of questions, the cross examination, included any questions that furthered the investigation or had anything to do with relevant circumstances or corroborative facts surrounding the case.

9. **False witnesses:** Hebrew law provided that any person bearing false witness would suffer the same penalty that the accused person would have suffered had the accused been found guilty.

10. **The accused as witness:** An accused person was never compelled to testify against himself, but was permitted and encouraged to offer testimony in his own behalf. Any testimony against one's self was accepted as evidence and considered in connection with other facts of the case. However, standing alone, a confession could never form the basis of a conviction.

11. **Relevancy of Hebrew evidence:** Both hearsay evidence and circumstantial evidence were irrelevant under Hebrew law.

12. **Antecedent warning:** When charged with a crime involving life and death, or punishable by corporal punishment, no person could be convicted unless he met specific, unusual guidelines. Competent testimony

must show that immediately before the commission of the crime, the offender was warned that he was about to commit a crime and that he would suffer a certain penalty for it. *And*, the warning was not valid if any time had elapsed between it and the crime.

Methods of Jewish Capital Punishment

Before Rome conquered Judea, the Great Sanhedrin had authority to impose capital punishment. After Judea became a client state to Rome, the Great Sanhedrin could carry out a death penalty only after receiving approval from Rome. When the Sanhedrin found Jesus guilty of blasphemy, the sentence of death that the Sanhedrin desired for him had to be approved by the Romans. It appears that at times the Hebrews were not patient enough to wait for Roman approval to carry out a death penalty. This was the case when Annas was deposed. The same may apply in the matter of the woman taken in adultery and in the stoning of the prophet Stephen.

Crucifixion was never practiced by the Jews. Even at the time they had authority over capital punishment, Jewish law allowed for only four options of execution: stoning, burning, beheading, or strangling. If a Jew were crucified, the act had to be carried out by the Romans.

Though crucifixion is often described as the most heinous method of execution, the four types of Jewish capital punishment were also distressingly painful.

1. **Beheading** was the punishment for two crimes: murder and communal apostasy. Though relatively merciful, this was considered the most awful of all forms of

punishment. It was carried out by fastening the culprit securely to a post, and severing his head from his body with a single stroke of a sword.

2. **Strangling** was prescribed for adultery with a married woman, wounding a parent, kidnapping a fellow Jew, false prophecy, and insubordination to the Sanhedrin. It was effected by burying the culprit waist deep in soft mud and then tightening a cord wrapped in a soft cloth around his neck until he suffocated.

3. **Burning** was the penalty for incest. But this Jewish method of execution differed from our modern notions of burning to death. As with strangling, the culprit was buried in soft mud, but for this method, buried *past* the waist. The culprit was suffocated with a cord wrapped around the neck. When the culprit lost consciousness and his jaw dropped open, a lighted wick (or, sometimes, molten lead) was quickly thrown into the mouth, constituting the burning.

4. **Stoning** was the penalty for at least 18 offenses and was the most common form of execution. Stoning offenses included blasphemy, cursing a parent, violating the Sabbath, and practicing magic. Stoning was a grizzly event. The victim was taken to a tall hill or cliff. (In Jerusalem, the stoning cliff was known as *Beth haSeqilah*, and was only about 11 feet high.) From the top of this precipice, the victim was thrown down by the first witness. The fall usually broke the neck and caused death. If death were not instantaneous, the second witness would cast upon the body a stone so large it usually

took two people to lift and heave. If this stone did not produce death, then a crowd of onlookers threw stones until the victim died. The apostle Luke recorded an attempted stoning of Christ, illustrating the first step in execution by stoning—casting the culprit off a hill: "And all they in the synagogue, when they heard these things, were filled with wrath, And rose up, and thrust him [Jesus] out of the city, and led him unto the brow of the hill whereon their city was built, that they might cast him down headlong [to stone him for blasphemy]. But he passing through the midst of them went his way" (Luke 4:28–30).

These four methods of execution were the only forms of capital punishment used by the ancient Hebrews. They never practiced crucifixion. However, in an effort to employ one last insult towards the criminal found guilty of idolatry and blasphemy, they did sometimes employ a posthumous indignity resembling crucifixion. After being stoned for these crimes, the criminal's body was hanged in public view as a means of rendering the offense more hideous.[19]

---

[19] Deuteronomy 21:22; Chandler, 91–101; Edersheim, 584–585

SIX

THE DAYS BEFORE PALM SUNDAY

John 11:47 ". . . for this man doeth many miracles."

During his short three-year ministry Jesus developed a large following, even among the Sanhedrin, the chief ruling body of Judea. But believing Christ's teachings caused serious internal conflict for any member of the Sanhedrin. ". . . among the chief rulers also many believed on him; but because of the Pharisees they did not confess him [Jesus], lest they should be put out of the synagogue: For they loved the praise of men more than the praise of God" (John 12:42–43).

Many who believed in Christ were afraid to confess it, while many who didn't believe feared his influence nonetheless. Towards the end of Christ's ministry his enemies' enmity towards him became severe. The Gospels record over 43 incidents where the Jewish leaders contemplated or attempted to do away with Christ before officially trying him. "And when the chief priests and Pharisees had heard his parables, they perceived that he spake of them [the Sanhedrin]. But when they sought to lay hands on him, they feared the multitude, because they [the multitude] took him for a prophet" (Matthew 21:45–46). In the end, Judas would betray his Lord in the dark secluded Garden of Gethsemane, where there would be no crowds to defend Jesus.

John records that the chief priests and Pharisees gathered to discuss the miracles of Jesus, and "Then from that day forth they took counsel together for to put him [Jesus] to death" (John 11:53).

Matthew is even a little more descriptive: "Then assembled together the chief priests, and the scribes, and the elders of the people, unto the palace of the high priest, who was called Caiaphas, And consulted that they might take Jesus by subtilty, and kill him" (Matthew 26:3–4).

The alternate translation from the Greek makes Matthew's above quoted verse even more ugly: "And *plotted* that they might take Jesus by *treachery* and *cunning*, and kill him." It is hard to comprehend the emotional pain Christ must have suffered knowing he had come into the world to save those very schemers, knowing of their fear and hatred of him, and knowing of the physical pain and suffering that lay before him.

This hostile environment surrounded Jesus during the last few weeks of his mortal life, intensifying as the Great Sanhedrin moved into deadly action against him after he raised Lazarus from the dead. This was one of Christ's most profound miracles. It is a simple story. It is a powerful story. Two sisters, Mary and Martha, sent Jesus a message that their brother Lazarus was sick. "Now Jesus loved Martha, and her sister, and Lazarus" (John 11:5). But he did not go immediately to the bedside of his sick friend. However, Christ knew that Lazarus would be all right in the end, for he revealed, ". . . This sickness is not unto death, but for the glory of God, that the Son of God might be glorified thereby" (John 11: 4). Christ knew that raising Lazarus would allow him to perform the ultimate miracle and further glorify his Father in Heaven.

Christ waited two full days before he announced to his disciples, ". . . Let us go into Judea again" (John 11:7). ". . . Our friend Lazarus sleepeth; but I go, that I may awake him out of sleep" (John 11:11). The disciples were justifiably concerned and objected to his return, since they *knew* that the Jews were trying to kill Jesus. Of course they did not want Jesus to travel where his life would be in danger. They questioned, ". . . Master, the Jews of late sought to stone thee; and goest thou thither again?" (John 11:8)

But Jesus returned to Bethany and ". . . found that he [Lazarus] had lain in the grave four days already" (John 11:17). "And many of the Jews came to Martha and Mary, to comfort them concerning their brother" (John 11:19).

Upon seeing him, both Martha and Mary exclaimed, ". . . Lord, if thou hadst been here, my brother had not died" (John 11:21, 32). And Mary fell at his feet and wept, and the Jews that had come to comfort her wept also. And "Jesus wept" (John 11:35). Then Jesus went to the grave, ordered the stone be removed, and "... cried with a loud voice, Lazarus, come forth" (John 11:43).

And in that glorious moment, "... he that was dead came forth, bound hand and foot with graveclothes: and his face was bound about with a napkin. Jesus saith unto them, Loose him and let him go" (John 11:44).

Many people witnessed this miracle and believed in Jesus Christ. "But some of them went their ways to the Pharisees, and told them what things Jesus had done. Then gathered the chief priests and the Pharisees a council [a quorum of at least 23], and said, What do we? for this man doeth many miracles. If we let him thus alone, all men will believe on him: and the Romans shall come and take away both our place and nation" (John 11:46–48).

The members of the Sanhedrin worried that they would no longer be the governing body. It is nearly unbelievable that these supposed men of God, the religious leaders of the people, were so eager to protect their own positions that they failed to appreciate the majesty and sacredness of the miracle that had just been performed by Christ and witnessed by a crowd. Instead of expressing grateful praise for the miraculous power of God, they expressed only selfish concern for the puny power of man.

One would expect a sudden, questioning hush to fall over the entire council when "... Caiaphas, being the high priest that same year, said unto them, Ye know nothing at all, Nor consider that it is expedient for us, that one man [Jesus Christ] should die for the people, and that the whole nation perish not. And this spake he not of himself: but being high priest that year, he prophesied that Jesus should die for that nation; and not for that nation only, but that also he should gather together in one the children of God that were scattered abroad" (John 11:49–52).

It seems bizarre that Caiaphas, the wicked chief high priest, whose family business desecrated the temple, would bear testimony to the council gathered before him that Jesus was the Great Redeemer who would die for all God's children. Nevertheless, it is significant that after such a bold statement from their leader, Caiaphas, ". . . from that day forth they took counsel together for to put him to death" (John 11:53).

Sadly, "Jesus therefore walked no more openly among the Jews . . . " (John 11:54). He led his most intimate disciples to the little town of Ephraim, about 20 miles north of Jerusalem, and explained his impending death and resurrection to those who would carry on his ministry.

Jesus had first spoken of his death and resurrection while ministering in Galilee. "From that time forth began Jesus to shew unto his disciples, how that he must go unto Jerusalem, and suffer many things of the elders and chief priests and scribes [the Sanhedrin], and be killed, and be raised again the third day" (Matthew 16:21). "And while they abode in Galilee, Jesus said unto them, The Son of man shall be betrayed into the hands of men: And they shall kill him, and the third day he shall be raised again. And they were exceeding sorry" (Matthew 17:22–23). Exceeding sorry! Naturally, his disciples would be sorry that Christ was to die. But because they could not fully comprehend the noble greatness of his mission as The Redeemer, their sorrow was not tempered by the joy that could have been associated with the miraculous events that were about to occur.

Mark records the Savior speaking of the same thing, "And he began to teach them, that the Son of man must suffer many things, and be rejected of the elders, and of the chief priests, and scribes, and be killed, and after three days rise again" (Mark 8:31).

". . . The Son of man is delivered into the hands of men, and they shall kill him; and after that he is killed, he shall rise the third day" (Mark 9:31).

As the Feast of the Passover approached, Christ surprised his disciples with his specific knowledge of the upcoming events, ". . . Behold, we go up to Jerusalem, and all things that are written by the prophets concerning the Son of man shall be accomplished" (Luke 18:31). ". . . and the Son of man shall be betrayed unto the chief priests and unto the scribes, and they shall condemn him to death, And . . ." (Matthew 20:18–19) ". . . he shall be delivered unto the Gentiles, and shall be mocked, and spitefully entreated, and spitted on: and they shall scourge him and put him to death: and the third day he shall rise again. And they understood none of these things . . . " (Luke 18:32–34).

While Christ was prophesying to his apostles about the upcoming events surrounding the feast days, many Jews, including the Sanhedrin, wondered whether Christ would return to Jerusalem again. "Now both the chief priests [mostly Sadducees] and the Pharisees had given a commandment, that, if any man knew where he [Jesus] were, he should shew it, that they might take him" (John 11:57). So eager were they to remove the threat of Christ, both the Sadducees and Pharisees *commanded* the people to disclose his whereabouts. The Sanhedrin had decided that it was a prudent time to capture Jesus—before the feast, while he was away from the multitudes that adored him.

Of course, as the feast days approached, Christ did return to Jerusalem, prepared to fulfill all prophecy.

SEVEN

THE TRIUMPHANT ARRIVAL

Matthew 21:9 "And the multitudes . . . that followed cried
saying, Hosanna . . ."

The Last Week

Friday, March 31, A.D. 34[20]
(six days before the Passover)

Christ arrived in Bethany in the late afternoon and lodged with Mary, Martha, and Lazarus.

---

[20] For reckoning and ease of picturing the time of the year, the author has chosen to refer to these dates according to comparisons to our own calendar. The actual dates remain a subject of discussion. This is also the date as we would note it, according to Edersheim, 619.

Saturday, April 1, A.D. 34
(five days before the Passover)

This was the last Sabbath of the Lord's mortal life. The gospel writers have drawn a reverential veil over this day, leaving us to presume that Christ spent it worshiping his Father and teaching his twelve apostles of their impending mission.

At the end of the day, when the Sabbath was formally over, Christ ate supper with the twelve apostles in the house of Simon the leper.[21] During this supper, Mary took ". . . a pound of ointment of spikenard, very costly, and anointed the feet of Jesus, and wiped his feet with her hair . . . " (John 12:3). Judas Iscariot,[22] one of the twelve apostles, objected to the anointing, declaring, "Why was not this ointment sold for three hundred pence, and given to the poor?" (John 12:5). Christ reprimanded him and told Judas that Mary had done a good thing, "For ye have the poor always with you; but me ye have not always" (Matthew 26:11).

Perhaps that simple reprimand from Jesus was the final motivation that Judas needed, to push him to his notorious deed. For at that point he ". . . went unto the chief priests, And said unto them, What will ye give me, and I will deliver him [Jesus] unto you? And they covenanted with him for thirty pieces of silver. And from that time he [Judas] sought opportunity to betray him" (Matthew 26:14–16).

Many Jews had gathered outside of the house of Simon to see the guests at supper. They were interested in seeing both

---

[21] Matthew 26:6 and Mark 14:3

[22] Judas was the only one of the twelve apostles who was not from Galilee.

Lazarus, who had been raised from the dead, and Christ, who had called Lazarus forth from the tomb.[23] Because of the people's great interest in both men, ". . . the chief priests consulted that they might put Lazarus also to death . . . " (John 12:10).

Sunday, April 2, A.D. 34
(four days before the Passover)

From Bethany, Christ and his disciples walked approximately three miles towards Jerusalem."And when they came nigh to Jerusalem . . . at the Mount of Olives, he sendeth forth two of his disciples, And saith unto them, Go your way into the village . . . and as soon as ye be entered into it, ye shall find a colt tied, whereon never man sat; loose him, and bring him. And if any man say unto you, Why do ye this? say ye that the Lord has need of him; and straightway he will send him hither" (Mark 11:1–3).

It happened exactly as Jesus said it would, and the two disciples brought the colt back. Then they put their coats on the donkey so that Jesus might sit upon it, just as Zechariah prophesied.[24] Many in the gathering crowd spread their garments on the ground before Jesus. Others cut branches off palm trees and spread them before the Christ. "And when he was come nigh, even now at the descent of the Mount of Olives, the whole multitude of the disciples began to rejoice and praise God with a loud voice for all the mighty works that they had seen . . . " (Luke 19:37). "And they that went before, and they that followed, cried,

---

[23] John 12:9
[24] Zechariah 9:9

saying, Hosanna;[25] Blessed is he that cometh in the name of the Lord: Blessed be the kingdom of our father David, that cometh in the name of the Lord: Hosanna in the highest. And Jesus entered into Jerusalem, and into the temple . . ." (Mark 11:9–11) In Matthew's record, the crowd actually called Christ "the son of David" (Matthew 21:9), a title reserved for the Messiah or Savior, indicating they now recognized him as the Christ come to deliver them.

When the crowd exclaimed, ". . . Blessed be the King that cometh in the name of the Lord . . . some of the Pharisees from among the multitude said unto him [Jesus], Master, rebuke thy disciples" (Luke 19:38–39). The Pharisees demanded that the Savior tell the crowd to stop calling him what he really was. To stop honoring and worshiping him.

Christ responded to the Pharisees with a fascinating answer, "I tell you that, if these should hold their peace, the stones would immediately cry out" (Luke 19:40). It was a moment for Christ, the very son of God, to be worshiped, a moment pregnant with adulation for the Son of man, the Redeemer of all mankind. Apparently, even the stones sensed this moment. How tragic that the Pharisees did not. If the multitude were forced into silence, the stones themselves would break the quiet and declare his divinity!

Later, Christ entered the temple, blessing and teaching his disciples. But beneath this inviting and hallowed moment in

---

[25] Meaning, "God save us now," similar to words used in Psalms 118:25. "An exclamation, originally an appeal to God for deliverance, used in praise of God or Christ." *Webster's Encyclopedic Unabridged Dictionary of the English Language* (New York City: dilithium Press, Ltd., 1989) 686.

the temple churned a darker certainty, the sacrifice required of a savior. Noting this darkness, Christ uttered the following poignant words, "Now is my soul troubled; and what shall I say? Father, save me from this hour: but for this cause have I come unto this hour" (John 12:27). Racked by the ultimate inner turmoil of a soul in anguish, Jesus Christ begged his Father to save him from the experience, the mission, for which he had been born. Though Christ *knew* that he must go through Gethsemane and Golgotha—that the fulfillment of his mission was imminent—he wanted to be saved from doing so. Of the countless lessons Christ taught us through word and deed, perhaps this is most important of all: No matter how difficult the job, the duty, the responsibility, the trial—*even the commandment*—no matter how much we fear it or don't want to fulfill it, we must learn to obey and do what is required of us by our Heavenly Father.

Christ continued, "Father, glorify thy name. Then came there a voice from heaven, saying, I have both glorified it, and will glorify it again. The people therefore, that stood by, and heard it, said that it thundered: others said, An angel spake to him" (John 12:28–29).

It is interesting that people heard the Father's message differently. Some said it thundered. Some said an angel had called out the pronouncement and testimony. And it is interesting that these 2000 years later, people still hear the Father's message differently. After this remarkable testimony from the Father, Jesus departed.

This episode in the temple made believers out of some: ". . . among the chief rulers also many believed on him; but because of the Pharisees they did not confess him, lest they should be put out of the synagogue: For they loved the praise of men more than the praise of God" (John 12:42–43).

"... and now the eventide was come, he [Jesus] went out unto Bethany with the twelve" (Mark 11:11). Christ's last Sunday on earth was over.

Monday, April 3, A.D. 34
(three days before the Passover)

The next day, on his return to Jerusalem, "... he hungered. And when he saw a fig tree in the way, he came to it, and found nothing thereon, but leaves only, and said unto it, Let no fruit grow on thee henceforward for ever. And presently [Greek: *immediately*] the fig tree withered away. And when the disciples saw it, they marveled, saying, How soon is the fig tree withered away! Jesus answered and said unto them, Verily I say unto you, If ye have faith, and doubt not, ye shall not only do this which is done to the fig tree, but also if ye shall say unto this mountain, Be thou removed, and be thou cast into the sea; it shall be done. And all things, whatsoever ye shall ask in prayer, believing, ye shall receive" (Matthew 21:18–22).

When Christ raised Lazarus from the dead, he demonstrated his power over death. The withering of the fig tree proclaims his power over life as well.

After Jesus and the disciples left the fig tree, "... they came to Jerusalem: and Jesus went into the temple, and began to cast out them that sold and bought in the temple, and overthrew the tables of the moneychangers, and the seats of them that sold doves; And would not suffer that any man should carry any vessel through the temple. And he taught, saying unto them, Is it not written, My house shall be called of all nations the house of prayer? but ye have made it a den of thieves" (Mark 11:15–17).[26]

"And the blind and the lame came to him in the temple; and he healed them. And when the chief priests and scribes saw the wonderful things that he did, and the children crying in the temple, and saying, Hosanna to the Son of David; they were sore displeased, And said unto him, Hearest thou what these say? And Jesus saith unto them, Yea; have ye never read, Out of the mouth of babes and sucklings thou hast perfected praise?" (Matthew 21:14–16)

Even before this day, the members of the Great Sanhedrin were angry with Christ and had already declared their fear of his powers and his influence over the people. After the worshipful display of the people when Christ rode into Jerusalem on a donkey, and after this second cleansing of the temple,[27] surely the Great Sanhedrin were roused beyond any prior anger or fear towards Christ. And with the cleansing of the temple, Christ became more than a political and theological enemy; he now posed an economic threat to the leaders of the Sanhedrin—the members of the House of Hanan, who sold the sacrificial doves and other animals in the temple.

At the end of the day, Christ walked back to Bethany.

---

[26] See also Matthew 21:12–13 and Luke 19:45–46

[27] It had been three years since he first drove the money changers out of the temple.

Tuesday, April 4, A.D. 34
(two days before the Passover)

On this day, Christ came to the temple for the last time. ". . . and as he was walking in the temple, there came to him the chief priests, and the scribes, and the elders . . . " (Mark 11:27). So all three quorums of the Great Sanhedrin (priests, scribes, and elders) were represented by those who approached Christ that day. They knew it would be unwise to try to take Jesus while he was in the midst of so many loyal followers, and had therefore devised a different plan. Believing their knowledge of the scriptures and the laws to be greater than that of this simple man from Galilee, they decided to debate him, hoping to trip him on his own words.

Their questioning began: ". . . By what authority doest thou these things? and who gave thee this authority to do these things?" (Mark 11:28) Two seemingly simple questions— loaded with deceit. Those members of the Sanhedrin thought that Christ's answers to their carefully worded questions would surely allow them to accuse Christ of blasphemy. Those that were questioning him had already witnessed signs of his power throughout his ministry. They were not doubting his power. Their questions dealt solely with his authority. By Jewish law, it was well understood that no one could take that authority unto himself. If Christ claimed no authority, he would be in conflict with Mosaic law. On the other hand, if he were to claim authority, not having received it from those who were questioning him, he would be accused of blasphemy.

No one appreciates more than a lawyer the importance of strategy. But these foolish men were dealing with the master strategist. Christ did not even deign to answer their questions. Instead, he immediately took control by asking a question of his own, ". . . I will also ask of you one question, and answer me, and I will tell you by what authority I do these things. The baptism of John, was it from heaven, or of men? answer me" (Mark 11:29–30).

Out-questioned, the priests conferred among themselves. They were not concerned with answering Christ correctly, but rather, answering in a way that would please the most people and, therefore, keep themselves safe. "And they reasoned with themselves, saying, If we shall say, From heaven; he will say, Why then did ye not believe him?" (Mark 11:31) "But and if we say, Of men; all the people will stone us: for they be persuaded that John was a prophet" (Luke 20:6).

Although they had foolishly assumed that they could trap Christ with difficult questions, at least now they demonstrated true wisdom by answering him with three simple words, "We cannot tell" (Mark 11:33).

Their reply was undoubtedly a bit more humble than their first probing questions had been. And considering their posture, they could not complain at the Lord's response: ". . . Neither do I tell you by what authority I do these things" (Mark 11:33).[28]

Immediately after his brilliant answer that confounded those who would harm him, Christ proceeded to relate a parable—pointedly defining the very men who were questioning

---

[28] See also Matt. 21:23–27; Mark 11:27–33; Luke 20:1–8

him. It was the parable of the man who sent his two sons to work in the vineyard.[29]

Directly after reciting this parable, Christ gave a warning unto the chief priests and elders who had been questioning him. He said, ". . . Verily I say unto you, That the publicans and harlots go into the kingdom of God before you. For John [the Baptist] came unto you in the way of righteousness, and ye believed him not: but the publicans and the harlots believed him: and ye, when ye had seen it, repented not afterward, that ye might believe him" (Matthew 21:31–32).

Immediately after rebuking those members of the Sanhedrin, Christ offered a second parable: The householder who planted a vineyard, and the wicked husbandmen who killed his servants and son.[30] "And when the chief priests and Pharisees had heard his parables, they perceived that he spake of them. But when they sought to lay hands on him, they feared the multitude, because they [the multitude] took him for a prophet" (Matthew 21:45–46).

Unchallenged, Christ chastened with still another, even more damning parable: The king who made a marriage feast for his son.[31]

Being afraid of openly taking him in front of the crowd, the Pharisees walked away and ". . . took counsel how they might entangle him in his talk" (Matthew 22:15). The Pharisees were determined to trick Christ into speaking treason. "And

---

[29] Matthew 21:28–32

[30] Matthew 21:33–41; also Mark 12:1–9, Luke 20:9–19

[31] Matthew 22:1–14

they watched him, and sent forth spies [Pharisees and Herodians], which should feign themselves just men, that they might take hold of his words . . . so they might deliver him unto the power and authority of the governor" (Luke 20:20).

So this little group of spies approached the Savior, pretending to be good men who were earnestly interested in the answers to their questions. They asked, ". . . Master, we know that thou art true, and teachest the way of God in truth . . . Tell us therefore, What thinkest thou? Is it lawful to give tribute unto Caesar, or not?" (Matthew 22:16–17)

It was indeed a clever question. The wrong answer could bring the instant accusation of treason. Anyone in the crowd around Christ who was truly interested in the answer likely pressed forward to more clearly hear his words. Those spies who posed the question were likely feeling incredibly sharp-witted, hoping to be credited with bringing to justice this bold man who called himself "Savior."

But the Lord's unexpected reply dashed those hopes when ". . . Jesus perceived their wickedness, and said, Why tempt ye me, ye hypocrites?" (Matthew 22:18) One can almost hear a frustrated sigh escape his lips when Christ directed, "Shew me the tribute money . . ." (Matthew 22:19).

Of course, everyone wondered why he would ask to see money. Surely he had seen it often enough. ". . . And they brought unto him a penny. And he saith unto them, Whose is this image and superscription?" (Matthew 22:19)

And surely Christ knew whose image was on the coin; he had seen it on coins and statues and flags innumerable times.

Still, ". . . They answered and said, Caesar's" (Luke 20:24). And then Christ uttered that remarkable response that still echoes through the ages, ". . . Render therefore unto Caesar the things which are Caesar's; and unto God the things which are God's" (Matthew 22:21). It has been over 2000 years since those words were spoken. It is doubtful that since that time a more powerful sermon has been delivered in such few words.

Probably most of those listening to Christ that day appreciated his clever response as far as it concerned Caesar—since Caesar's image was on the coin it would not be a violation of Jewish law to pay over the tribute money to Caesar. But Christ's symbolism could also be interpreted at a much deeper level. As Caesar had his image stamped on his coins, so likewise ". . . God created man in his own image, in the image of God created he him; male and female created he them" (Genesis 1:27). With God's image upon *us*, perhaps we have the obligation to render our lives to God—as did the Jews with their tribute money to Caesar.

The Pharisees and Herodians who had originally come to ". . . catch him in his words" (Luke 12:13) recognized the astute answer Christ had given, for "When they had heard these words, they marvelled, and left him, and went their way" (Matthew 22:22).

As if in competition with the Pharisees to disarm the Savior, "The same day came to him the Sadducees, which say that there is no resurrection, and asked him," (Matthew 22:23) in parable form, a question dealing with the resurrection. Their parable (involving the woman who was married to seven successive brothers)[32] was a ruse to cover their real question of him: Is there a resurrection?

Again, Jesus demonstrated his discernment and quiet brilliance against those who would confuse and convict him. He wisely recounted verses of scripture to prove his point. He pronounced, "And as touching the dead, that they rise: have ye not read in the book of Moses, how in the bush God spake unto him, saying, I am the God of Abraham, and the God of Isaac, and the God of Jacob? He is not the God of the dead, but the God of the living: ye therefore do greatly err" (Mark 12:26–27). It was a profound message. So simple! When God spoke to Moses—declaring himself God of Abraham, Isaac, and Jacob—the three prophets he mentioned were long dead. Yet he still avowed being their God. The obvious conclusion was that death is not the end . . . *we still live.*

"And when the multitude heard this, they were astonished at his doctrine" (Matthew 22:33). And when the Pharisees (who held to strict observance of the law) heard that Jesus Christ had silenced the Saducees, they gathered together and "Then one of them, which was a lawyer [a scribe], asked him a question, tempting him, and saying, Master, which is the great commandment in the law?" (Matthew 22:35–36).

Which is the great commandment? It was a significant question. The Jews had so many commandments that no matter which one Christ would choose, they could catch him by showing how another may be more important. But these foolish men

---

[32] Matthew 22:25–28

were questioning the very *author* of the commandments—the scriptures. Once again, the perfect answer sprang to Christ's lips. A message that would be repeated millions of times and thousands of years hence. "Jesus said unto him, Thou shalt love the Lord thy God with all thy heart, and with all thy soul, and with all thy mind. This is the first and great commandment. And the second is like unto it, Thou shalt love thy neighbor as thyself" (Matthew 22:37–39).

Christ had defined not only the first and great commandment for the questioning Pharisees, he volunteered the second as well. The scribes, Pharisees, Sadducees, and Herodians combined could not refute him. The lawyer that had asked the question responded, ". . . Well, Master, thou hast said the truth: for there is one God; and there is none other but he: And to love him with all the heart, and with all the understanding, and with all the soul, and with all the strength, and to love his neighbor as himself, is more than all whole burnt offerings and sacrifices" (Mark 12:32–33).

Jesus then avowed that this lawyer answered independently of the others with his remark, and he assured the scribe, ". . . Thou art not far from the kingdom of God" (Mark 12:34).

Christ's answers that day to those religious leaders who were determined to trip him up were so profound that ". . . neither durst any man from that day forth ask him any more questions" (Matthew 22:46).

When Christ left the temple that Tuesday and began his journey back to Bethany, he stopped to rest near the summit of the Mount of Olives. He taught his apostles about the devastating calamities that would precede his second coming.[33] He gave his poignant farewell to Jerusalem. His heartfelt words define his feelings: "O Jerusalem, Jerusalem, thou that killest the prophets, and stonest them which are sent unto thee, how often would I have gathered thy children together, even as a hen gathereth her chickens under her wings, and ye would not! Behold, your house is left unto you desolate. For I say unto you, Ye shall not see me henceforth, till ye shall say, Blessed is he that cometh in the name of the Lord" (Matthew 23:37–39). And finally, he pronounced his last three parables: the ten virgins,[34] the talents,[35] and the sheep and goats.[36]

Wednesday, April 5, A.D. 34
(one day before the Passover)

Christ spent the day with the twelve in Bethany. He presumably gave them further instructions to prepare them for the time shortly to come when he would be no more with them.

And as the Feast of the Passover drew nigh, ". . . the chief priests and scribes sought how they might kill him; for they feared the people" (Luke 22:2).

Thursday, April 6, A.D. 34
(The Passover)

This day marked the true beginning of the end in the mortal life of our Lord and Savior Jesus Christ. This day would

---

[33] Matthew 24
[34] Matthew 25:1–13
[35] Matthew 25:14–30
[36] Matthew 25:31–46

bring the institution of the sacrament of the Lord's Supper. It would bring a whole new concept of pain and suffering into the world, a concept laced in red . . . a Gethsemane. This day would unmask the worst traitor the world had ever known or would ever know.

This day, love and forgiveness and obedience and sacrifice would weave together in a miraculous tapestry that would free mankind from sin and error by opening a conduit to the very heavens, a conduit available to all mankind. But this amazing day started like any other . . . .

Food was a concern. However, unlike other days, this food involved a sacred Jewish holiday. "Now the first day of the Feast of Unleavened Bread the disciples came to Jesus, saying unto him, Where wilt thou that we prepare for thee to eat the passover?" (Matthew 26:17) Then Christ gave his disciples specific directions on how and where to find the "upper room."

EIGHT

THE LAST SUPPER, THE BETRAYAL, AND THE ARREST

Luke 22:48 ". . . betrayest thou the Son of man with a kiss?"

"Now when the even was come, he [Jesus] sat down with the twelve" (Matthew 26:20). All four Gospels agree that the Passover supper was the first event of the evening. And the four Gospels generally agree on the events that comprise the rest of the night. A few of the following occurrences that take place that evening are listed in slightly different order within the four Gospels, and some events are not recorded in every

Gospel. When all four Gospels are considered, the following is a brief synopsis of Thursday night:[37]

"And as they sat and did eat, Jesus said, Verily I say unto you, one of you which eateth with me shall betray me. And they began to be sorrowful, and to say unto him one by one, Is it I? and another said, Is it I?" (Mark 14:18–19) This room of 13 men had shared much during the previous three years. Lodgings, boat rides, storms, meals, and miracles. They had witnessed the gentle Jesus defending and loving the little children, feeding the hungry, and befriending even the untouchables—the lepers. They had heard the sincere Jesus devoutly professing his new ideas on love and forgiveness, honesty and hypocrisy. They had seen the righteous anger of the indignant Jesus, clearing the temple, the very house of his Father. And the miracles, over and over. Now their Master announced that one of them would betray him.

In his Gospel record, John the Beloved allows us a peek into the tender relationship that existed between the Savior and one of the Apostles. Still wondering who among them would betray their Lord, ". . . the disciples looked one on another, doubting on whom he [Jesus] spake. Now there was leaning on Jesus' bosom one of his disciples, whom Jesus loved. Simon Peter therefore beckoned to him, that he should ask who it should be of whom he spake. He then lying on Jesus' breast saith unto him, Lord, who is it?" (John 13:22–25)

And Christ answered the question of his beloved apostle, ". . . He that dippeth his hand with me in the dish, the same

---

[37] See Matthew 26:19–75; Mark 14:17–72; Luke 14–71; John 13:1–38 and 18:1–27

shall betray me" (Matthew 26:23). Judas was seated in the place of honor at the left hand of Christ.[38]

"Then Judas, which betrayed him, answered and said, Master, is it I? He [Jesus] said unto him, Thou hast said" (Matthew 26:25), meaning "You yourself said it" or "It is as thou hast said." In other words He said, "Yes, you are the one who will betray me." With three simple words, "Thou hast said," Christ acknowledged to Judas that he knew who the betrayer was; that it was indeed Judas himself.

Either before the Passover meal, or when dinner was over, the apostles were made clean as Jesus took a towel and poured ". . . water into a basin and began to wash the disciples' feet, and to wipe them with the towel . . ." (John 13:5). This was a common thing for a servant to do because in the days of Christ people walked dusty roads that covered their feet with the grime of travel. When guests entered a house, it was customary for a servant to wash their feet for them. The disciples must have been astounded when Jesus did so.

---

[38] "We know from the Gospel narrative that John occupied the place on His right, at that end of the divans—as we may call it—at the head of the table. But the chief place next to the Master would be that to His left, or above Him. In the strife of the disciples, which should be accounted the greatest, this had been claimed, and we believe it to have been actually occupied, by Judas. This explains how, when Christ whispered to John by what sign to recognize the traitor, none of the other disciples heard it. It also explains, how Christ would first hand to Judas the sop, which formed part of the Paschal ritual, beginning with him as the chief guest at the table, without thereby exciting special notice. Lastly, it accounts for the circumstance that, when Judas, desirous of ascertaining whether his treachery was known, dared to ask whether it was he, and received the affirmative answer, no one at the table knew what had passed. But this could not have been the case, unless Judas had occupied the place next to Christ; in this case, necessarily that at His left, or the post of chief honour." Edersheim, 494

However, when Jesus came to Peter, "Peter saith unto him, Thou shalt never wash my feet" (John 13:8). Peter seemed appalled at the thought of Jesus kneeling before him to perform the menial job of a servant. But he quickly changed his attitude when "Jesus answered him, If I wash thee not, thou hast no part with me" (John 13:8). Both men had expressed bold statements on the matter. But Peter immediately retracted his words and humbly exposed his great love of the Savior by exclaiming, ". . . Lord, not my feet only, but also my hands and my head" (John 13:9). It is a sweet show of devotion from both men and illustrates how each child of God must accept the humble, atoning sacrifice made by the Greatest of All, or have no part of its fruit, forgiveness.

After he washed the feet of the apostles, the Savior administered the first sacrament of the Lord's supper, "And he took bread, and gave thanks, and break it, and gave unto them, saying, This is my body which is given for you: this do in remembrance of me. Likewise also the cup after supper, saying, This cup is the new testament [Greek: *covenant*] in my blood, which is shed for you" (Luke 22:19–20).

At some point in the evening, ". . . the devil having now put into the heart of Judas Iscariot, Simon's son, to betray him [Christ] . . ." (John 13:2). ". . . Satan entered into him [Judas]. Then said Jesus unto him, That thou doest, do quickly" (John 13:27). It is hard to comprehend that Judas left the room after such a pointed farewell. Christ might have been saying, "Do it quickly! Get it over with! Go and betray me, your Savior, your Master who has just washed your feet, who has just shared with you the Passover meal and has just administered the first sacrament, who will shortly hang on the cross for you. Do it quickly!" Yes, that is hard to comprehend. Yet even considering the pain caused by the traitor Judas, Christ was careful to not openly expose him to the other apostles. No one at the table knew why the Lord told Judas to "do it quickly."

Even when Judas left the room, the others assumed he left to take care of some purchases for the feast or some other task related to his being in charge of the money bag.[39]

After the dinner, the foot washing, and the administration of the sacrament, the little group of men in that upper room sang a hymn. Envisioning them singing together helps to humanize them, these men whom the Lord had chosen to be his special representatives during his lifetime . . . and after. Perhaps the Savior knew they would all need that special spiritual lift that comes when singing hymns. "And when they had sung an hymn [presumably one of the Passover hymns[40]], they went out into the Mount of Olives.[41] Then saith Jesus unto them, All ye shall be offended because of me this night . . . " (Matthew 26:30–31).[42]

Upon hearing his Master predict that the apostles' would be offended because of him that same night, Peter boldly

---

[39] John 12:6; 13:29

[40] "The hymn, with which the Paschal supper ended, had been sung. Probably we are to understand this of the second portion of the Hallel (Psalms 113–118), sung sometime after the third Cup, or else of Psalm 136, which in the present ritual, stands near the end of the service." Edersheim, 533.

[41] Luke 22:39 reads "And he [Jesus] came out [of the upper room] and went, as he was wont [Greek: accustomed], to the Mount of Olives." Evidently, Jesus often went to the Mount of Olives (Gethsemane was an olive orchard).

[42] See also Mark 14:26–27

declared, ". . . Though all men shall be offended because of thee, yet will I never be offended" (Matthew 26:33). Jesus responded with haunting words to Peter's assertion of loyalty, ". . . I tell thee, Peter, the cock shall not crow this day, before that thou shalt thrice deny that thou knowest me" (Luke 22:34).

By his reply it is obvious that Peter could not imagine a situation in which he would deny the Lord. For, "Peter said unto him, Though I would die with thee, yet will I not deny thee. Likewise also said all the disciples" (Matthew 26:35). All eleven apostles pronounced they would die for him before they would deny him. They could not imagine the horrors to which their beloved Jesus would soon be exposed.

Either in the upper room or on the Mount of Olives, Christ delivered one last sermon to his apostles.[43] He gave the new commandment that they love one another, he again foretold of his death, he offered a discourse on the Holy Ghost, and he prayed to the Holy Father for his apostles: ". . . Holy Father, keep through thine own name those whom thou hast given me . . . I kept them in thy name: those that thou gavest me I have kept, and none of them is lost, but the son of perdition [Judas] . . . I pray . . . that thou shouldest keep [the rest of] them from the evil" (John 17:11–12, 15).

The pivotal point of the day—and of the history of mankind—was about to transpire. Christ finished talking to his disciples on the Mount of Olives, and ". . . he went forth with his disciples over the brook Cedron, where was a garden [Gethsemane], into the which he entered, and his disciples"

---

[43]John, chapters 13–17

(John 18:1). And Jesus ". . . saith unto the disciples, Sit ye here, while I go and pray yonder. And he took with him Peter and the two sons of Zebedee [James and John], and began to be sorrowful and very heavy [Greek: *began to be distressed and troubled*]. Then saith he unto them, My soul is exceeding sorrowful, even unto death: tarry ye here, and watch [Greek: *stay awake*] with me" (Matthew 26:36–38).

Already Christ seems to be experiencing the pain so shortly before him, his soul sorrowful unto death. And although his travail in the Garden seems to have required solitude, he still sought the companionship of his apostles, asking them to stay awake with him.

Of all the Gospels, John's touches least on Christ's suffering in Gethsemane. Matthew and Mark provide more detailed narratives of Christ's experience in the Garden. After he told Peter, James, and John to watch with him, Christ ". . . went a little further and fell on his face, and prayed, saying, O my Father, if it be possible, let this cup pass from me: nevertheless not as I will [Greek: *wish, desire*], but as thou wilt" (Matthew 26:39). Mark records Christ pleading with the Father slightly differently, ". . . Abba, Father, all things are possible unto thee; take away this cup from me: nevertheless not what I will, but what thou wilt" (Mark 14:36).

It is Luke, the doctor, who allows a deeper insight into Christ's experience in the Garden, including three additional details which the other Gospel authors didn't mention. Luke's first addition is only a matter of physical detail. He tells us that when Christ left Peter, James, and John ". . . he was withdrawn from them about a stone's cast . . ." (Luke 22:41). His second addition is more significant. He relates that "... there appeared an angel unto him from heaven, strengthening him" (Luke 22:43). Certainly this angel supported the Savior during that painful moment when he asked for the cup to pass from him. But Luke's third addition is his most significant, opening our eyes to Christ's purpose in the Garden: "And being in an agony he prayed more earnestly: and his sweat was as it were great drops of blood falling down to the ground" (Luke 22:44). An agony this intense must signify that Christ's purpose in the Garden was not limited to praying for help. Surely, as some noted scriptorians have suggested, at least *part* of the atonement took place in the Garden of Gethsemane. Theologian James Talmage writes:

> Christ's agony in the garden is unfathomable by the finite mind, both as to intensity and cause. The thought that He suffered through fear of death is untenable. Death to Him was preliminary to resurrection and triumphal return to the Father from whom He had come, and to a state of glory even beyond what He had before possessed; and, moreover, it was within His power to lay down His life voluntarily. He struggled and groaned under a burden such as no other being who has lived on earth might even conceive as possible. It was not physical pain, nor mental anguish alone, that caused Him to suffer such torture as to produce an extrusion of blood from every pore; but a spiritual agony of soul such as only God was capable of experiencing.

No other man, however great his powers of physical or mental endurance, could have suffered so; for his human organism would have succumbed, and syncope[44] would have produced unconsciousness and welcome oblivion. In that hour of anguish Christ met and overcame all the horrors that Satan, 'the prince of this world' could inflict . . . .

"From the terrible conflict in Gethsemane, Christ emerged a victor. Though in the dark tribulation of that fearful hour He had pleaded that the bitter cup be removed form His lips, the request, however oft repeated, was always conditional; the accomplishment of the Father's will was never lost sight of as the object of the Son's supreme desire. The further tragedy of the night, and the cruel inflections that awaited Him on the morrow, to culminate in the frightful tortures of the cross, could not exceed the bitter anguish through which He had successfully passed."[45]

Three times Christ withdrew to pray, and three times he returned to Peter, James, and John and found them asleep; they slept through most of the Lord's painful ordeal. Evidently, Christ had to do this alone. Upon his third return, being gentle with them, he uttered, ". . . Sleep on now, and take your rest:

---

[44] *Syncope:* A fainting, or loss of consciousness, caused by a temporary deficiency of blood supply to the brain

[45] Talmage, James E., *Jesus the Christ* (Salt Lake City: Deseret Book Company, 1962) 613

behold, the hour is at hand, behold, and the Son of man is betrayed into the hands of sinners" (Matthew 26:45). But when flickering lights in the distance betrayed the arrival of the betrayer himself, Christ knew that the apostles' rest was over and exclaimed, "Rise, let us be going: behold, he is at hand that doth betray me" (Matthew 26:46).

The Betrayal and Arrest

From past personal experience with the Lord, Judas suspected that Christ would retire to the Garden of Gethsemane after the Passover meal. "And Judas also, which betrayed him, knew the place [Gethsemane]: for Jesus ofttimes resorted thither with his disciples" (John 18:2). The dark deceit of Judas was thorough; he betrayed his Master by using information he had gained as a disciple, an intimate, familiar with Christ's personal life.

Judas was so confident that Christ would retire to the Garden that he brought with him to Gethsemane ". . . a great multitude with swords and staves, from the chief priests and the scribes and the elders" (Mark 14:43). ". . . and captains of the temple, and . . ." (Luke 22:52) ". . . a band of men and officers from the chief priests and Pharisees . . . with lanterns and torches and weapons" (John 18:3).

The captains of the temple, mentioned by Luke, were controlled by the Sanhedrin, so their inclusion indicates the Sanhedrin's explicit involvement in the scheme to arrest Jesus. John informs us that "a band of men" approached with Judas. The Greek word for "band" is "cohort," a unit which numbers from 300–600 men and is one of ten divisions in a Roman

Legion.[46] This information leads us to believe that Pilate must have given approval to the use of his soldiers in arresting Jesus. All figured, there may have been as many as 600 men in the weapon-wielding mob that beset the unarmed Christ that quiet night. Many of those men arrived anxious for blood, unaware of the innocent blood that had already stained the now holy ground.

"And he [Judas] that betrayed him had given them [the crowd] a token, saying, Whomever I shall kiss, that same is he; take him, and lead him away safely" (Mark 14:44). ". . . and forthwith he came to Jesus, and said, Hail, master; and kissed him" (Matthew 26:49). And the Savior's response echos his own deep sadness as he both questions and condemns the evil betrayer, ". . . Judas, betrayest thou the Son of man with a kiss?" (Luke 22:48).

John's Gospel gives us a deeper view of the poignant scene played out in the Garden. When Judas and the crowd entered the Garden, armed with torches and weapons, "Jesus therefore, knowing all things that should come upon him, went forth, and said unto them, Whom seek ye? They answered him, Jesus of Nazareth. Jesus saith unto them, I am he. And . . . they went backward, and fell to the ground" (John 18:4–6). Whatever caused their fall, Christ's presence had quite an impact on the mob.

Obviously in control of the situation, Christ ". . . asked he them again, Whom seek ye? And they said, Jesus of Nazareth" (John 18:7). Then Christ, who only moments ago was shedding

---

[46] *Webster's Encyclopedic Unabridged Dictionary of the English Language,* 289.

great drops of his own blood, demonstrated his love and concern for his apostles, pronouncing, ". . . I am he: if therefore ye
seek me, let these [the apostles] go their way . . . ." (John 18:8).

The apostles, likewise, were least concerned for themselves. "When they which were about him saw what would
follow, they said unto him, Lord, shall we smite with the
sword?" (Luke 22:49). Their courage and faith is especially
admirable considering the size of their opposition.

About this time, the impetuous ". . . Simon Peter having a
sword drew it, and smote the high priest's servant, and cut off
his right ear . . ." (John 18:10). Although one's heart might cheer
for Peter's defense of the Lord, the Master himself touched the
man's ear and healed him and then replied in reprimand.
"Then said Jesus unto him, Put up again thy sword into its
place . . . Thinkest thou that I cannot now pray unto my Father,
and he shall presently give me more than twelve legions of
angels?"[47] (Matthew 26:53) That could be the hardest trial that
Christ had to endure: Knowing that at any time, at any point,
he could summon the protection of tens of thousands of angels.
During the entire 24-hour ordeal, minute by minute—even second by second—Christ knew that he could instantly free himself from the exquisite physical and emotional pain that was
Gethsemane . . . and the trials . . . and Golgotha.

Then Jesus turned to the crowd and boldly declared, ". . .
Are ye come out as against a thief with swords and staves for
to take me? I sat daily with you teaching in the temple, and ye

---

[47] A Roman legion included up to 6,000 men, so as many as 72,000 angels
could have been called to fight.

laid no hold on me" (Matthew 26:55). How foolish that crowd must have felt, a huge group of soldiers and religious leaders armed with weapons of death in order to capture this one gentle man who taught of peace and love and turning the other cheek, this carpenter from Galilee who had healed the blind, the lame, and the deaf, this humble Nazarene who had raised the dead.

". . . Then all the disciples forsook him, and fled" (Matthew 26:56).

"Then the band and the captain and officers of the Jews took Jesus, and bound him, And led him away to Annas first . . . " (John 18:12–13). The illegal trial, the mockery of justice, was about to begin.

NINE

THE ILLEGAL HEBREW TRIALS

Matthew 26:65 ". . . what further need have we of witnesses?"

Christ was tried in four distinct trials—two under Hebrew jurisdiction and two under Roman law. Immediately before the first trial, Christ was taken to the palace of Annas, where he was unofficially questioned in a private examination. From there, Christ was moved to the palace of Caiaphas—chief high priest of the Sanhedrin—where the first trial took place late Thursday night. The second trial occurred early Friday morning, at an unknown location, possibly still at the palace of Caiaphas. It took place before a quorum, at least 23 members of the Sanhedrin. The third, and best documented trial took place before Pilate, procurator of Judea. And it was Pilate who sent him to his fourth trial to appear in front of Herod Antipas, tetrarch of Galilee. Herod Antipas sent Christ back to Pilate; thus, the trial before Pilate actually consisted of two parts. Not one of the players, save Christ himself, knew that he was to be participating in the most famous criminal trial in the history of the world.

The Questioning at the Palace of Annas

From Gethsemane, Christ was led to the palace of Annas. As a past chief high priest of the Great Sanhedrin, Annas had remained powerful through his son-in-law Caiaphas, who was the reigning chief high priest. As noted in Chapter Two, Annas was a wicked and adulterous leader, one of the wealthiest and most powerful and influential Jews in Jerusalem. The simple fact that Christ was brought to Annas first is significant. Annas, who many referred to as "God's high priest," was figuratively giving his stamp of approval on the proceedings that were to follow. Though this interrogation by Annas was unofficial, that Christ should even be brought before him virtually assured Christ the ultimate penalty of death. Christ's death may have been more the fault of Annas and Caiaphas than of anyone else. While speaking to Pilate, Christ himself may have referred to one or both of them when he asserted, ". . . he that delivered me unto thee hath the greater sin" (John 19:11).

"The high priest [Annas] then asked Jesus of his disciples, and of his doctrine" (John 18:19). Christ knew the Jewish law. He knew that under the law, a charge or accusation must be brought by a witness. So "Jesus answered him, I spake openly to the world; I ever taught in the synagogue, and in the temple, whither the Jews always resort; and in secret have I said nothing. Why askest thou me? ask them which heard me, what I have said unto them: behold, they know what I said" (John 18:20–21). It was a fair answer. Jesus had never skulked around in dark places, preaching civil disobedience. He preached openly—to any who would listen, and was often heard by members of the Sanhedrin.

Despite the logic and legality of the Savior's reply, he was abruptly chastised for it. "And when he had thus spoken, one of the officers which had stood by struck Jesus with the palm of his hand, saying, Answerest thou the high priest so?" (John 18:22).

But Christ hadn't been insolent; he had simply pointed out that Annas was obligated to follow the correct procedures of Jewish law. "Jesus answered him, If I have spoken evil, bear witness of the evil: but if well, why smitest thou me?" (John 18:23) Christ knew he was well within his rights. Under Jewish law, a person could not be required to testify against himself, and, furthermore, two witnesses were required for any conviction of an illegal act. Christ questioned why the officer should smite him for merely asking for his legal rights.

Apparently Annas saw that he couldn't answer Christ, so he ". . . sent him bound unto Caiaphas the high priest" (John 18:24).

These early hours of Christ's trials frame one of the most poignant stories of the Bible. It began in Gethsemane. When Christ was led away by the soldiers, ". . . Peter followed him afar off unto the high priest's palace, and went in, and sat with the servants, to see the end" (Matthew 26:58).

Peter had entered a courtyard, possibly one that connected the palaces of Annas and Caiaphas. As he sat by a fire's warmth, a maid of the high priest ". . . looked upon him, and said, And thou also wast with Jesus of Nazareth. But he denied saying, I know not, neither understand I what thou sayest . . ." (Mark 14:67–68). Then a servant of the high priest, a relative of the man whose ear Peter had severed, asked Peter, ". . . Did not I see thee in the garden with him? Peter then denied again . . ." (John 18:27).

About an hour later, a man confidently declared of Peter, ". . . Of a truth, this fellow also was with him: for he is a Galilaean. And Peter said, Man, I know not what thou sayest. And immediately, while he yet spake, the cock crew" (Luke 22:59–60). It seems that at this precise moment Christ was being led through that common outer courtyard between the palace of Annas and Caiaphas, for the next verse reads: "And the Lord turned, and looked upon Peter. And Peter remembered the word of the Lord, how he had said unto him, Before the cock crow, thou shalt deny me thrice" (Luke 22:61).

It is hard to imagine Peter's remorse in that painful moment of fulfilled prophesy. Overcome, ". . . Peter went out, and wept bitterly" (Luke 22:62).

The Jewish Trial at the Palace of Caiaphas

After passing Peter, Christ was led to the palace of Caiaphas. We do not know how many members of the Sanhedrin convened that night, but Mark 14:53 informs us: ". . . they led Jesus away to the high priest: and with him were assembled all the chief priests and the elders and the scribes"

(Mark 14:53). It seems highly likely that a quorum (at least 23 members) of the Sanhedrin had gathered in the palace of Caiaphas, waiting for Jesus to be brought before them. They seemed to have known that Christ would be arrested that night and that they needed a crime with which to charge him. Under the direction of the chief high priest, Caiaphas, this little group of hypocritical leaders of the Jews was trying to arrange a legal method to do away with Jesus Christ.

At the time of the trial of Jesus, it was the duty of the presiding officer of the court to call the attention of the witnesses to the value of life, and to warn those witnesses not to forget anything they knew in the prisoner's favor. It seems the chief high priest forgot that responsibility completely, determining to do exactly the opposite.

"Now the chief priests, and the elders, and all the council, sought false witness against Jesus, to put him to death; But found none . . . " (Matthew 26:59–60). Right from the beginning, members of the Sanhedrin were looking for trumped up charges against Christ. They wanted him dead—no matter how they had to arrange it. But their willingness to use deceitful charges was to no avail, "For many bare false witness against him, but their witness agreed not together" (Mark 14:56).

Jesus *listened* to their accusations, but did not reply. "And the high priest arose and said unto him, Answerest thou nothing?" (Matthew 26:62). But Christ continued to listen in silence,[48] as was his legal right.

---

[48] Matthew 26:63

In reality, had the Sanhedrin been able to produce the proper witnesses, they *may* have been able to prove Christ guilty of blasphemy, since performing wonders and miracles or forgiving sin—without due credit to Jehovah—were acts of blasphemy under Jewish law.[49] Of course, *Christ* did not have to give verbal credit to Jehovah . . . he *was* Jehovah. He was the only living person who could *not* be guilty of that particular charge of blasphemy. He was indeed the Son of God, the Savior of mankind.

Not knowing, or acknowledging, that Christ was the Son of God, one easily could have judged him guilty of blasphemy according to Jewish law. Among Christ's observers and followers were many who could have supported such a charge:

1. The scribe who had heard Jesus forgive sins.[50]

2. Those who saw Jesus cast out devils.[51]

3. Jarius, whose daughter Jesus raised from the dead.[52]

4. The widow of Nain, whose son Jesus raised from the dead.[53]

5. Any of the thousands that Jesus fed with five loaves and two fishes.[54]

---

[49] When Moses smote the rock twice and water gushed out, he did not credit the Lord for this miracle. This brought him under condemnation and kept him from entering the promised land. (Numbers 20:10–12)

[50] Matthew 9:2

[51] Mark 7:25–30

[52] Luke 8:41–42, 49–56

[53] Luke 7:12–15

[54] Matthew 14:15–21; Mark 6:35–44; Luke 9:12–17; John 6:5–14

But the Great Sanhedrin had not found any legitimate witness, and Christ chose to listen in silence to their absurd accusations. His silence, however legal, seemed to rouse the high priest, who illegally called upon Jesus to testify against himself: "... I adjure thee [Greek: *charge (you) under oath*] by the living God, that thou tell us whether thou be the Christ, the Son of God" (Matthew 26:63).

"And Jesus said, I am: and ye shall see the Son of man sitting on the right hand of power, and coming in the clouds of heaven" (Mark 14:62).

Then the high priest Caiaphas, in an illegal act of grave frustration or anger, tore his cloak, "... saying, He hath spoken blasphemy; what further need have we of witnesses? behold, now ye have heard his blasphemy. What think ye? They answered and said, He is guilty of death" (Matthew 26:65–66).

This overly dramatic act of coat rending was especially deplorable because it made the manner of polling the Sanhedrin notably illegal. Correct procedure dictated that the vote be taken in order—from the most junior to the most senior member. The high priest, who should have voted last, had burst out with an obvious vote of guilty by rending his coat. By that act, he knew he would get the vote he wanted. He was assured total affirmation of his guilty verdict.

And these members of the Great Sanhedrin had performed yet another illegal act: declaring Christ guilty of death, *urging his death in an illegal trial!* Yet these were the men who were responsible to try him on the morrow. Having already determined him guilty, surely they should have been dismissed with extreme prejudice from the proceedings. But that did not happen.

We do not know how long into the early morning hours Christ was abused in the first trial. He who could call down legions of angels stood quietly as ". . . they spit in his face, and buffeted him; and others smote him with the palms of their hands . . . " (Matthew 26:67). "And when they had blindfolded him, they struck him on the face, and asked him, saying, Prophesy, who is it that smote thee?" (Luke 22:64) Ironically, only a few days earlier, the Savior had prophesied of this very humiliation. While on his way to Jerusalem, he had told his apostles that the Son of man would be taken, "And they shall mock him, and shall scourge him, and shall spit upon him, and shall kill him: and the third day he shall rise again" (Mark 10:34). The mocking had begun; the killing was yet to come. And through the greatness and love of God . . . so was the rising again.

Friday, April 7, A.D. 34
(Day of the Crucifixion)
The Second Jewish Trial

In a disingenuous effort to appear as though they were conducting Christ's trial legally, the Great Sanhedrin declared that the trial be held the next morning at the proper time (between sunrise and sundown), and perhaps in the proper place (the Chamber of Hewn Stone), and under proper leadership (a full quorum). So the next day, "When the morning was come, all the chief priests and elders of the people [the Sanhedrin] took counsel against Jesus to put him to death . . . " (Matthew 27:1). In spite of the laws that they professed to follow and cherish, this was not to be a legal trial. The judges were seeking witnesses *against* him instead of appointing council *for* him. The entire Sanhedrin proceeded to condemn Jesus, wanting him put to death. Though the high priest had already pronounced him guilty of blasphemy the night before, on this morning they ". . . led him into their council, saying, Art thou the Christ? tell us. And he said unto them, If I tell you, ye will not believe . . . " (Luke 22:66–67). Of course, Christ was right—the sham trial of the night before had proven his assertion. The Sanhedrin wanted the Savior dead, no matter who or what he was.

Even knowing they would not believe, Christ answered their question, saying, "Hereafter shall the Son of man sit on the right hand of the power of God" (Luke 22:69). But the Sanhedrin wanted a more precise answer, "Then said they all, Art thou then the Son of God? And he said unto them, Ye say that I am" (Luke 22:70). Mark recorded a more direct answer when Christ was asked, ". . . Art thou the Christ, the Son of the Blessed? And Jesus said, I am: and ye shall see the Son of man sitting on the right hand of power, and coming in the clouds of heaven" (Mark 14:61–62). The Sanhedrin became enraged with the simple truth of Christ's reply. "And they said, What need we any further witness? for we ourselves have heard of his own mouth" (Luke 22:71).

Though this should have been the greatest trial in all history, it had not been even a semblance of a trial. No evidence of misdeed was presented. No defense was allowed. This entire group of highly trained scriptorians refused to give any credence to the man or the numerous prophecies which he had undoubtedly fulfilled. This alleged trial was merely a short council, with a predetermined conclusion. All too quickly, the entire Sanhedrin arose, "And when they had bound him, they led him away, and delivered him to Pontius Pilate the governor" (Matthew 27:2).

TEN

THE ILLEGALITIES OF THE HEBREW TRIALS

John 18:14 ". . . it was expedient that one man should die . . . "

After arresting Jesus in the Garden of Gethsemane, the Great Sanhedrin filled the following 24 hours with flagrant violations of the Rules of Procedure and Rules of Witnesses and Evidence that defined Hebrew trials, as examined in Chapter Three. Even the nighttime arrest of Jesus was illegal, violating rule #1 of Rules of Procedure: "Proceedings [including an arrest] were to be held during the day; no process was allowed to begin at night." The following rules also were violated during the Hebrew trials of Christ, some of them were violated several times—each occurrence a distinct breach of Hebrew law:

Hebrew Rules Violated When Jesus Was Questioned at the Palace of Annas

1. **Jesus was questioned at night.** Violated Rules of Procedure, #1: Proceedings were to be held during the day; no process was allowed to begin at night.

2. **Jesus was taken to the palace of Annas.** Violated Rules of Procedure, #3: Proceedings were to be held only in the Chamber of Hewn Stones [a temple chamber].

    This questioning took place at the palace of Annas.

3. **Jesus was not questioned before a quorum.** Violated Rules of Procedure, #5: At least 23 members of the Great Sanhedrin were required to form a quorum that would try a case.

    A quorum was not assembled. Annas was sitting in the unofficial capacity as sole judge, and he was not even the chief high priest. It was a private examination before the beginning of the regular trial.

4. **Jesus was questioned on the day of a Passover Feast and on the eve of a Jewish Sabbath.** Violated Rules of Procedure, #8: No proceedings could be held on Sabbaths or feast days **or** on the *eves* of Sabbaths or feast days.

    The Passover officially began at sunset on Thursday; therefore, the last supper, which was held on Thursday night, was part of the Passover celebration. Since Jewish days span from sunset to sunset, Thursday night was also the eve of the Sabbath that would begin at sunset on Friday.

5. **The accusation of Jesus was based on the testimony of an accomplice, Judas.** Violated Rules of Witnesses and Evidence, #3: Number required to convict: Under Hebrew law, an accusing witness, together with two eyewitnesses, were required for a conviction.

   Though Judas bargained to betray Christ, he could not legally serve as the prosecuting—or accusing—witness because he was a participant in the blasphemy of which Christ was accused. Judas could not be considered the witness who originated, or made, the charges. Since Judas was one of the twelve apostles who was so heavily involved in the daily activities of Christ, he was considered an accomplice to any crime of which the Sanhedrin would find Christ guilty.

6. **The indictment of Jesus was originated by the Sanhedrin.** Violated Rules of Procedure, #9: Sanhedrin members could not originate charges nor could they witness against the accused.

   A complaining witness, not the Sanhedrin, should have initiated the complaint.

7. **Jesus was taken before a prejudiced judge.** Violated Rules of Procedure, #7: Prejudiced judges could not participate in the trial.

   Annas was the patriarch of the House of Hanan, which sold sacrificial animals within the temple grounds. Because Jesus preached against such sales, Annas had an economic interest in the outcome of this trial.

8. **Jesus was convicted on the basis of his own testimony and not that of any other witness.** Violated Rules of Procedure, #10: Hebrew Rules of Witnesses and Evidence had to be maintained. And rule #10 of Witnesses and Evidence stated: The accused as witness: An accused person was never compelled to testify against himself, but was permitted and encouraged to offer testimony in his own behalf. Any testimony against one's self was accepted as evidence and considered in connection with other facts of the case. However, standing alone, a confession could never form the basis of a conviction.

    In the palace of Annas, there were no witnesses against Christ. When Annas asked Christ about his doctrine, Annas illegally used the Savior's testimony to convict him.

9. **Jesus asked for an accusing witness—as was his right by law—and was denied.** Violated Rules of Procedure, #3: Number required to convict: Under Hebrew law, an accusing witness, together with two eyewitnesses, were required for a conviction.

    Jesus had always been very open about his teachings. When the high priest asked him about his doctrine, "Jesus answered him, I spake openly to the world; I ever taught in the synagogue, and in the temple, whither the Jews always resort; and in secret I said nothing. Why askest thou me? ask them which heard me, what I have said unto them: behold, they know what I said" (John 18:20–21). Christ knew the Hebrew laws. When he stated, "ask them which heard me," he was merely asking for a witness—*as was his right*. He knew that two eyewitnesses and an accusing witness were required to convict. But the Sanhedrin never produced *one* credible witness.

Hebrew Rules Violated When Jesus Was Tried at the Palace of Caiaphas (The First Jewish Trial)

1. **Jesus was tried by Caiaphas and the Sanhedrin at night.** Violated Rules of Procedure, #1: Proceedings were to be held during the day; no process was allowed to begin at night.

2. **Jesus was taken to the palace of Caiaphas.** Violated Rules of Procedure, #3: Proceedings were to be held only in the Chamber of Hewn Stones [a temple chamber].

   This alleged trial took place at the residence of Caiaphas; thus, the sentence of condemnation was pronounced in a place forbidden by law.

3. **Jesus was tried on the day of a Passover Feast and on the eve of a Jewish Sabbath.** Violated Rules of Procedure, #8: No proceedings could be held on Sabbaths or feast days or on the *eves* of Sabbaths or feast days.

   The Passover officially began at sunset on Thursday; thus, the last supper, which was held on Thursday night, was part of the Passover celebration. Since Jewish days span from sunset to sunset, Thursday night was also the eve of the Sabbath that would begin at sunset on Friday.

4. **The accusation of Jesus was based on the testimony of an accomplice, Judas.** Violated Rules of Procedure, #3: Number required to convict: Under Hebrew law, an accusing witness, together with two eyewitnesses, were required for a conviction.

    Though Judas bargained to betray Christ, he could not legally serve as the prosecuting—or accusing—witness because he was a participant in the blasphemy of which Christ was accused. Judas could not be considered the witness who originated, or made, the charges. Since Judas was one of the twelve apostles who was so heavily involved in the daily activities of Christ, he was considered an accomplice to any crime of which the Sanhedrin would find Christ guilty.

5. **Jesus had not yet been charged. The indictment of Jesus was originated by the Sanhedrin. The Sanhedrin actively sought a complaining witness.** Violated Rules of Procedure, #9: Sanhedrin members could not originate charges, nor could they witness against the accused.

    The Sanhedrin sought witnesses against Christ. A complaining witness, not the Sanhedrin, should have initiated the complaint.

6. **Jesus was taken before prejudiced judges.** Violated Rules of Procedure, #7: Prejudiced judges could not participate in the trial.

    Like his father-in-law, Annas, Caiaphas had an economic interest in the outcome of this trial. So did many other members of the Sanhedrin. Even beyond the money issue, Caiaphas was not an impartial judge; he had an interest in the outcome of the trial. He had previously declared about the accused, ". . . it is expedient for us, that one man [Jesus Christ] should die for the people, and that the whole nation perish not" (John 11:50). He was obviously predisposed to the death of Jesus Christ. Because of his disposition to have Christ put to death (John 11:50), Caiaphas should have been disqualified.

7.   **The testimonies of the witnesses against Jesus did not agree together.** Violated Rules of Witnesses and Evidence, #6: Agreement of Witnesses: The witnesses were required to agree on all essential details. If not, their testimonies were rejected as invalid.

   The Sanhedrin knowingly heard false witnesses, but the testimonies of those witnesses disagreed and in this case they were correctly rejected as legally invalid.

8.   **The merits of the defense of Jesus were not considered.** Violated Rules of Procedure, #11: The merits of a defense had to be heard.

   Absolutely no defense was offered during this trial of Christ, although numerous points could have been made. (See Chapter Eleven "Merits of the Defense.")

9.   **The Rules of Witnesses and Evidence were not maintained.** Violated Rules of Procedure, #10: Hebrew Rules of Witnesses and Evidence had to be maintained. (See list of Rules of Witnesses and Evidence.)

10. **The high priest rent his clothes.** Violated Rules of Procedure, #12: No rending of clothes was allowed.

    During this trial, when asked by Caiaphas, Jesus proclaimed himself the son of God. At that point, Caiaphas rent his clothes. Though it was an illegal act, it certainly conveyed to those assembled exactly how Caiaphas stood on the subject. It was his signal that he felt the defendant was guilty. Obviously, his dramatic display could not be ignored by the other members of the Sanhedrin.

11. **Jesus was convicted on his uncorroborated confession.** Violated Rules of Witnesses and Evidence, #10: The accused as witness: An accused person was never compelled to testify against himself, but was permitted and encouraged to offer testimony in his own behalf. Any testimony against one's self was accepted as evidence and considered in connection with other facts of the case. However, standing alone, a confession could never form the basis of a conviction.

    When Caiaphas asked Christ if he was the son of God, Christ answered in the affirmative. Christ bore witness that he was the son of God, to which Caiaphas proclaimed, ". . . what further need have we of witnesses?" (Matthew 26:65) However, Caiaphas and the Sanhedrin did have need of further witnesses, simply because this was a requirement of the law.

12. **The balloting was irregular.** Violated Rules of Procedure, #13: A vote determined the verdict. Seated around the table

or room in order of seniority, beginning with the most recently appointed, members voted on the charges.

The vote at this trial was not taken from most junior member to the senior member. At the conclusion of the trial, when Caiaphas asked the members of the Sanhedrin for a verdict, they unanimously replied, ". . . He is guilty of death" (Matthew 26:66). The lawful method of voting one at a time had given way to mob mentality.

13. **Jesus was convicted with a unanimous verdict of guilty.** Violated Rules of Procedure, #14: A unanimous verdict of guilty had the same effect as an acquittal.

After the Sanhedrin unanimously pronounced that Christ was guilty of death, he should have been set free. And because a sentence of capital punishment could not be passed on the day of the trial, the decision of the judges should have been reexamined on the following day, instead of just after the pronouncement of guilt. (Rule #15)

Hebrew Rules Violated At the Early Morning Trial of Jesus Before the Sanhedrin (The Second Jewish Trial)

1. **Jesus was tried before the morning sacrifice had been offered.** Violated Rules of Procedure, #2: Proceedings could be held only after the morning sacrifice at the temple.

2. **Jesus was tried on the day of a Passover Feast and on the eve of a Jewish Sabbath.** Violated Rules of Procedure, #8:

No proceedings could be held on Sabbaths or feast days or on the *eves* of Sabbaths or feast days.

The Passover officially began at sunset on Thursday; thus, the last supper, which was held on Thursday night, was part of the Passover celebration. Since Jewish days span from sunset to sunset, Thursday night was also the eve of the Sabbath that would begin at sunset on Friday.

3. **The accusation of Jesus was based on the testimony of an accomplice, Judas.** Violated Rules of Witnesses and Evidence, #3: Number required to convict: Under Hebrew law, an accusing witness, together with two eyewitnesses, were required for a conviction.

    Though Judas bargained to betray Christ, he could not legally serve as the prosecuting—or accusing—witness because he was a participant in the blasphemy of which Christ was accused. Judas could not be considered the witness who originated, or made, the charges. Since Judas was one of the twelve apostles who was so heavily involved in the daily activities of Christ, he was considered an accomplice to any crime of which the Sanhedrin would find Christ guilty.

4. **The indictment of Jesus was originated by the Sanhedrin.** Violated Rules of Procedure, #9: Sanhedrin members could not originate charges nor could they witness against the accused.

    A complaining witness, not the Sanhedrin, should have initiated the complaint.

5. **Jesus was taken before prejudiced judges.** Violated Rules of Procedure, #7: Prejudiced judges could not participate in the trial.

    Like his father-in-law, Annas, Caiaphas had an economic interest in the outcome of this trial. So did most of the other members of the Sanhedrin. Even beyond the money issue, Caiaphas was not an impartial judge. He had previously declared about the accused, ". . . it is expedient for us, that one man [Jesus Christ] should die for the people, and that the whole nation perish not" (John 11:50). He was obviously predisposed to the death of Jesus Christ.

6. **The merits of the defense of Jesus were not considered.** Violated Rules of Procedure, #11: The merits of a defense had to be heard.

    Absolutely no defense was offered during this trial of Christ. But numerous points could have been made. (See Chapter Eleven "Merits of the Defense")

7. **The Rules of Witness and Evidence were not maintained.** Violated Rules of Procedure, #10: Hebrew Rules of Witness and Evidence had to be maintained.

8. **Jesus was convicted on his uncorroborated confession.** Violated Rules of Witnesses and Evidence, #10: The accused as witness: An accused person was never compelled to testify against himself, but was permitted and encouraged to offer testimony in his own behalf. Any testimony against one's self was accepted as evidence and considered in

connection with other facts of the case. However, standing alone, a confession could never form the basis of a conviction.

Early this day, the Sanhedrin led Christ into their council. "Then said they all, Art thou then the Son of God? And he said unto them, Ye say that I am. And they said, What need we any further witness? for we ourselves have heard of his own mouth" (Luke 22:70–71). However, the Sanhedrin did have need of further witness, simply because this need was written into the law.

9.   **The balloting was irregular.** Violated Rules of Procedure, #13: A vote determined the verdict. Seated around the table or room in order of seniority, beginning with the most recently appointed, members voted on the charges.

The vote at this trial was not taken from most junior member to the senior member. There plainly was no vote, just a mob shouting, ". . .What need we any further witness? for we ourselves have heard of his own mouth" (Luke 22:71).

10. **Jesus was convicted with a unanimous verdict of guilty.** Violated Rules of Procedure, #14: A unanimous verdict of guilty had the same effect as an acquittal.

(If the vote were unanimous against the defendant, the judges were deemed prejudiced against him, as if the defendant's fate had been predetermined.)

When Caiaphas spoke to the Sanhedrin, asking, "Ye have heard the blasphemy: what think ye? And they all [note the *all*] condemned him to be guilty of death" (Mark 14:64). The result of that unanimous guilty verdict should have been immediate acquittal. Christ should have been set free.

11. **There was no time for the members of the Sanhedrin to fast before this trial.** Violated Rules of Procedure, #16: If two trials were needed, the judges were required to fast and pray between them.

    Because the Hebrew trials of Christ were illegally held on the same day (from sunset to sunset), there was no time to fast between them. Ignoring the parameters of the Jewish "day," it could be argued, weakly, that the trials were held on two different days. But the members of the Sanhedrin left the first trial very late at night (after dinner) and came back very early in the morning (before breakfast) (Luke 22:66). A few hours sleep can hardly qualify as a fast. It barely allowed time for a heartfelt prayer.

12. **Both of the Hebrew trials of Christ took place within one day.** Violated Rules of Procedure, #15: If a death sentence were pronounced, a second trial was to be held the following day.

    Under Jewish law, a day started at sunset and ended at sunset the next day. Any person tried and found guilty of a capital offense had to be given a second trial the following day. In the case of Christ, the arrest, the questioning at the palace of Annas, the trial at the palace of Caiaphas, and the early morning trial before the Sanhedrin all must have been completed within less than eight hours—from very late Thursday night to very early Friday morning. Under Hebrew reckoning, these events all took place on the same day. Though this council made the pretense of reconvening for the obligatory second-day trial, it was not the second day, and there was no second hearing. The Friday morning meeting was only a sham, an empty shell. It was merely a formal opportunity for the Sanhedrin to condemn Christ to death. No witnesses. No defense. No accuser.

ELEVEN

MERITS OF THE DEFENSE

Matthew 26:56 "But all this was done, that the scriptures of the prophets might be fulfilled."

Throughout the Hebrew trials of Christ, those in power insti-
gated many wicked actions or made many stupid mistakes.
Whether by accident or by brilliant deviousness, the leaders of
the Sanhedrin denied Christ one important opportunity that
should have been his under Jewish law. Though the Rules of
Procedure clearly stated that "The merits of a defense had to be
heard," not one word was heard on Christ's behalf.

But had he been given the chance, just who could this
humble man from Galilee have brought to his defense? In
Gethsemane, only a few hours earlier, Christ himself had
declared that if he prayed, his Father would send him ". . . more

than twelve legions of angels . . . " (Matthew 26:53). Some 72,000 angels would surely have convinced even the most hardened heart of the heavenly power of the Son of man.

And beyond his godly powers, in a fair trial in full daylight, Christ could have called before his judges a host of witnesses who were friendly to him. The following list describes many of the witnesses who could have been summoned to testify in Christ's defense:

1. **Mary, the virgin mother of Christ (if women had been allowed to testify).** The angel Gabriel was sent from God and announced to Mary the miraculous news, ". . . behold, thou shalt conceive in thy womb, and bring forth a son, and shalt call his name JESUS. He shall be great, and shall be called the Son of the Highest . . . And he shall reign over the house of Jacob for ever . . . " (Luke 1:31–32). This humble young woman responded with an innocent question that portrayed her virtue, ". . . How shall this be, seeing I know not a man? And the angel answered and said unto her, The Holy Ghost shall come upon thee, and the power of the Highest shall overshadow thee: therefore also that holy thing which shall be born of thee shall be called the Son of God" (Luke1:34–35).

2. **Bartimaeus, a blind man healed by Christ.** While he sat by the highway, begging, blind Bartimæus had called out, ". . . Jesus, thou Son of David, have mercy on me . . . . And Jesus answered and said unto him, What wilt thou that I should do unto thee? The blind man said unto him, Lord, that I might receive my sight.

And Jesus said unto him, Go thy way; thy faith hath made thee whole. And immediately he received his sight, and followed Jesus . . ." (Mark 10:47, 51–52).

3. **The Roman centurion whose servant was healed of the palsy.** A centurion had asked Jesus to heal his servant of palsy. "And Jesus saith unto him, I will come and heal him. The centurion answered and said, Lord, I am not worthy that thou shouldest come under my roof: but speak the word only, and my servant shall be healed" (Matthew 8:7–8). And Jesus answered the centurion, ". . . I have not found so great faith, no, not in Israel . . . . Go thy way; and as thou hast believed, so be it done unto thee. And his servant was healed in the selfsame hour" (Matthew 8:10, 13).[55]

4. **The son of the widow of Nain, who Christ raised from the dead.** Seeing a widow following in the funeral procession after her dead son—her only son—Christ had comforted her: ". . . Weep not. And he came and touched the bier: and they that bare him stood still. And he said, Young man, I say unto thee, Arise. And he that was dead sat up, and began to speak . . . " (Luke 7:13–15).

5. **Jarius, whose daughter Christ raised from the dead.** Seeking Christ's healing touch, Jarius, a ruler of the synagogue, had fallen at Christ's feet and begged the Lord to come and heal his only daughter. But by the time Jarius and Christ had reached the young girl, she had already died. As the girl's parents wept, Christ

---

[55] See also Luke 7:1–9

responded with gentle words, ". . . Weep not; she is not dead, but sleepeth . . . . And he . . . took her by the hand, and called, saying, Maid, arise. And her spirit came again, and she arose straightway . . . " (Luke 8:52, 54–55).

6. **Peter, James and John, Apostles who heard God the Father speak.** Jesus had taken Peter, James, and John up a high mountain (the mount of Transfiguration), where the four of them were alone. And Jesus ". . . was transfigured before them: and his face did shine as the sun, and his raiment was white as the light. And . . . behold, a bright cloud overshadowed them: and behold a voice out of the cloud, which said, This is my beloved Son, in whom I am well pleased; hear ye him" (Matthew 17: 2–3, 5).[56]

7. **Malchus, the temple guard whose severed ear was restored by Christ.** In an effort to defend Christ from arrest in the Garden of Gethsemene, ". . . Simon Peter having a sword drew it, and smote the high priest's servant, and cut off his right ear" (John 18:10). "And Jesus . . . touched his ear, and healed him" (Luke 22:51).

8. **Nicodemus, a member of the Sanhedrin, who had witnessed some of Christ's miracles.** One night Nicodemus had come to Jesus and declared, ". . . Rabbi, we know that thou art a teacher come from God: for no man can do these miracles that thou doest, except God be with him" (John 3:2). As a member of the Sanhedrin, the voice of Nicodemus held some weight.

---

[56] See also Mark 9:1–9

It is no wonder that he was not invited to speak in the Lord's defense.

9. **Lazarus, who Christ called forth from the tomb.** At peril of his own life, Jesus had traveled to the home of his sick friend, Lazarus. But by the time Christ arrived, Lazarus has been dead four days and laid to rest in a cave. After demanding that the stone in front of the cave be removed, Jesus looked heavenward, thanking and praising God, then ". . . cried with a loud voice, Lazarus come forth. And he that was dead came forth . . . " (John 11:43–44).

10. **The many that witnessed the raising of Lazarus from the tomb.** Before Christ had arrived at the home of Lazarus, ". . . many of the Jews came to Martha and Mary, to comfort them concerning their brother" (John 11:19). Those Jews wept with Mary, followed her to the grave, and witnessed the miracle of life returning to Lazarus.

11. **The hundreds that Christ had healed.** The deaf. The dumb. The blind. The lame. The palsied. The leprous. The crippled. The diseased.

12. **The thousands who were miraculously fed.** When Jesus had found himself surrounded by thousands of hungry followers, he was concerned that their lack of food might cause them to faint on the way home. He asked his apostles, ". . . How many loaves have ye? And they said, seven, and a few little fishes" (Matthew 15:34). After Christ blessed the meager food, it was broken and passed to the crowd of 4,000 men and an

unspecified number of women and children. Seven baskets full were left over. Another time, Jesus repeated this miracle using "... five barley loaves, and two small fishes ... " (John 6:9). This time, 12 baskets of food remained. "Then those men, when they had seen the miracle that Jesus did, said, This is of a truth that prophet that should come into the world" (John 6:14).

13. **The hundreds who were present at the baptism of Christ and heard God the Father speak.** "Now when all the people were baptized, it came to pass, that Jesus also being baptized, and praying, the heaven was opened, And the Holy Ghost descended in a bodily shape like a dove upon him, and a voice came from heaven, which said, Thou art my beloved Son; in thee I am well pleased" (Luke 3:21–22).

14. **Those present at the Temple who heard God the Father speak.** Only a few days before his trials, the day he made his triumphal entry into Jerusalem on the back of a donkey, Christ had been preaching in the temple and proclaimed, "Father, glorify thy name. Then came there a voice from heaven, saying, "I have both glorified it, and will glorify it again" (John 12:28). Many people had heard those words from the voice of God the Father.

The testimonies of the above witnesses would have clearly pronounced the divinity of the Lord. But instead, because of priestcraft, because the members of the Sanhedrin were afraid that Rome would come and take away their place and their nation, the Sanhedrin totally ignored their own laws concerning the merits of the defense. They convicted the only person living for whom it would be impossible to be guilty of the charge of blasphemy, the charge of taking upon himself the name of God.

Fulfillment of Prophecy

Testimonies of the witnesses could also have established the exact fulfillment of certain ancient Messianic prophesies about Christ's birth, life, arrest, and trial. Prophecies found in the very scriptures to which the Sanhedrin so adamantly professed to adhere. Some of these prophecies and the fulfillment of them include:

1.   The Messiah was to be born in Bethlehem.

Old Testament prophecy—Micah 5:2: "But thou, Bethlehem . . . out of thee shall he come forth unto me that is to be ruler in Israel; whose goings forth have been from of old, from everlasting."

New Testament fulfillment—Luke 2:4–7: "And Joseph also went up from Galilee, out of the city of Nazareth, into Judea, unto the city of David, which is called Bethlehem (because he was of the house and lineage of David:), To be taxed with Mary his espoused wife, being great with child. And so it was, that, while they were there, the days were accomplished that she should be delivered. And she brought forth her firstborn son, and wrapped him in swaddling clothes, and laid him in a manger; because there was no room for them in the inn."

2.   The Messiah was to be born of a virgin.

Old Testament prophecy—Isaiah 7:14: "Therefore the Lord

himself shall give you a sign; Behold, a virgin shall conceive, and bear a son, and shall call his name Immanuel [Hebrew: *With us is God*]."

New Testament fulfillment—Luke 1:26–27, 30–31, 34–5: "And . . . the angel Gabriel was sent from God unto a city of Galilee, named Nazareth, To a virgin espoused to a man whose name was Joseph, of the house of David; and the virgin's name was Mary. And the angel said unto her, Fear not, Mary: for thou hast found favour with God. And, behold, thou shalt conceive in thy womb, and bring forth a son, and shalt call his name JESUS. Then said Mary unto the angel, How shall this be, seeing I know not a man? And the angel answered and said unto her, The Holy Ghost shall come upon thee, and the power of the Highest shall overshadow thee: therefore also that holy thing which shall be born of thee shall be called the Son of God."

3.   The Messiah was to spring from the house of David.

Old Testament prophecy—Jeremiah 23:5–6: "Behold, the days come, saith the Lord, that I will raise unto David a righteous Branch, and a King shall reign and prosper . . . . and this is his name whereby he shall be called, THE LORD OUR RIGHTEOUSNESS."

New Testament fulfillment—Matthew 1:20: ". . . behold, the angel of the Lord appeared unto him in a dream, saying, Joseph, thou son of David, fear not to take unto thee Mary thy wife: for that which is conceived in her is of the Holy Ghost."

The New Testament records the conclusive fulfillment of that prophecy in the first 16 verses of the first chapter of Matthew. Those 16 verses trace the genealogy of Joseph, the stepfather of Jesus Christ, directly to King David. Mary also was a descendant of King David. "A personal genealogy of Joseph was essentially that of Mary also, for they were cousins."[57]

4. **The Messiah was to be called out of Egypt.**

Old Testament prophecy—Hosea 11:1: "When Israel was a child, then I loved him, and called my son out of Egypt."

New Testament fulfillment—Matthew 2:14–15: "When he [Joseph] arose, he took the young child and his mother by night, and departed into Egypt: And was there until the death of Herod: that it might be fulfilled which was spoken of the Lord by the prophet, saying: Out of Egypt have I called my son."

5. **The Messiah was to have a forerunner like unto Elijah to prepare the way.**

Old Testament prophecy—Malachi 3:1: "Behold I will send my messenger, and he shall prepare the way before me: and the Lord, whom ye seek, shall suddenly come to his temple, even the messenger of the covenant . . . ."

Old Testament prophecy—Isaiah 40:3: "The voice of him that crieth in the wilderness, Prepare ye the way of the Lord, make straight in the desert a highway for our God."

New Testament fulfillment—Matthew 3:1–3: "In those days came John the Baptist, preaching in the wilderness of Judea, And saying, Repent ye: for the kingdom of heaven is at hand. For this is he that was spoken of by the prophet Esaias [Isaiah],

---

[57] Talmage, 86

saying, The voice of one crying in the wilderness, Prepare ye the way of the Lord, make his paths straight." John the Baptist was foreordained to prepare the way and to baptize Jesus Christ.

6.   The Messiah was to begin his ministry in Galilee.

Old Testament prophecy—Isaiah 9:1–2: "Nevertheless the dimness shall not be such as was in . . . Galilee of the nations. The people that walked in darkness have seen a great light: they that dwell in the land of the shadow of death, upon them hast the light shined."

New Testament fulfillment—Matthew 4:12, 14, 16–17: "Now when Jesus had heard that John was cast into prison, he departed into Galilee . . . That it might be fulfilled which was spoken by Esaias [Isaiah] the prophet, saying . . . The people which sat in darkness saw great light; and to them which sat in the region and shadow of death light is sprung up. From that time Jesus began to preach, and to say, Repent: for the kingdom of heaven is at hand."

7.   The Messiah was to perform many miracles.

Old Testament prophecy—Isaiah 35:5–6: "Then the eyes of the blind shall be opened, and the ears of the deaf shall be unstopped. Then shall the lame man leap as an hart, and the tongue of the dumb sing: for in the wilderness shall waters break out, and streams in the desert."

Dozens of miracles were performed by Christ and recorded in the New Testament. Here are two:

New Testament fulfillment—Matthew 12:22: "Then was brought unto him one possessed with a devil, blind, and dumb: and he healed him, insomuch that the blind and dumb both spake and saw."

New Testament fulfillment—Matthew 11:2–5: "Now when John had heard in the prison the works of Christ, he sent two of his disciples, And said unto him, Art thou he that should come, or do we look for another? Jesus answered and said unto them, Go and shew John again those things which ye do hear and see: The blind receive their sight, and the lame walk, the lepers are cleansed, and the deaf hear, the dead are raised up, and the poor have the gospel preached to them."

8. **The Messiah was to make his public entry into Jerusalem riding upon an ass.**

Old Testament prophecy—Zechariah 9:9: "Rejoice . . . O daughter of Jerusalem: behold, thy King cometh unto thee: he is just, and having salvation; lowly, and riding upon an ass, and upon a colt the foal of an ass."

New Testament fulfillment—Matthew 21:6–9: "And the disciples went, and did as Jesus commanded them, And brought the ass, and the colt, and put on them their clothes, and they set him thereon. And a very great multitude spread their garments in the way; others cut down branches from the trees, and strewed them in the way. And the multitudes that went before, and that followed, cried, saying, Hosanna to the Son of David: Blessed is he that cometh in the name of the Lord; Hosanna in the highest."

9. **The Messiah was to be a man of suffering and was to be despised and rejected of men.**

Old Testament prophecy—Isaiah 53:3–4: "He is despised and rejected of men; a man of sorrows, and acquainted with grief: and we hid as it were our faces from him; he was despised, and we esteemed him not. Surely he hath borne our griefs, and carried our sorrows: yet we did esteem him stricken, smitten of God, and afflicted."

New Testament fulfillment—Luke 9:58: "And Jesus said unto him, Foxes have holes, and birds of the air have nests; but the Son of man hath not where to lay his head."

New Testament fulfillment—Mark 15:19–20: "And they smote him on the head with a reed, and did spit upon him, and bowing their knees worshiped him. And when they had mocked him, they took off the purple from him, and put his own clothes on him, and led him out to crucify him."

10. **The Messiah was to be betrayed by one of his followers for thirty pieces of silver which would be cast unto the potter in the house of the Lord.**

Old Testament prophecy—Psalms 41:9: "Yea, mine own familiar friend, in whom I trusted, which did eat of my bread, hath lifted up his heel against me" [the betrayal of Judas].

Old Testament prophecy—Zachariah 11:12–13: "And I said unto them, If ye think good, give me my price; and if not, forbear. So they weighed for my price thirty pieces of silver. And the Lord said unto me, Cast it unto the potter: a goodly price that I was prised of them. And I took the thirty pieces of silver, and cast them to the potter in the house of the Lord."

New Testament fulfillment—Matthew 26:14–16: "Then one of the twelve, called Judas Iscariot, went unto the chief priests, And said unto them, What will ye give me, and I will deliver him [Jesus] unto you? And they covenanted with him for thirty pieces of silver. And from that time he sought opportunity to betray him."

New Testament fulfillment—Matthew 27:3–7: "Then Judas, which had betrayed him, when he saw that he was condemned, repented himself, and brought again the thirty pieces of silver to the chief priests and elders, Saying, I have sinned in that I have betrayed the innocent blood. And they said, What is that to us? [Greek: *that is your affair*] see thou to that. And he [Judas] cast down the pieces of silver in the temple, and departed, and went and hanged himself. And the chief priests took the silver pieces, and said, It is not lawful for to put them into the treasury, because it is the price of blood. And they took counsel, and bought with them the potter's field, to bury strangers in."

There are several points of fascinating symbolic significance in the betrayal by Judas. This *friend* of Christ who betrayed our Lord was paid by the chief priest out of the temple money. The temple money had been reserved for the purchase of sacrifices. It is ironic that temple funds purchased Christ—Christ, who was the ultimate sacrifice.

And the agreed upon price of 30 pieces of silver was no accident. At that time, the price of a servant was 30 pieces of silver.[58] Christ took upon him the form of a servant and was purchased for 30 pieces of silver. Then our Lord and Savior, through his

---

[58] See Exodus 21:28–32

suffering at Gethsemane and Golgotha, purchased the freedom of all of us from the servitude and bondage of sin. He purchased the freedom and salvation of all who believe on him.

11. The Messiah was to be scourged,[59] shamed, and spit upon.

Old Testament prophecy—Isaiah 50:6: "I gave my back to the smiters, and my cheeks to them that plucked off the hair: I hid not my face from shame and spitting."

New Testament fulfillment—Matthew 27:26, 30: ". . . and when he [Pilate] had scourged Jesus, he delivered him to be crucified . . . . And they spit upon him . . . ."

New Testament fulfillment—Mark 14:65: "And some began to spit on him, and to cover his face, and to buffet him, and to say unto him, Prophesy: and the servants did strike him with the palms of their hands."

12. The Messiah was to be crucified.

Old Testament prophecy—Zechariah 13:6: "And one shall say unto him, What are these wounds in thine hands? Then he shall answer, Those with which I was wounded in the house of my friends."

Old Testament prophecy—Psalms 22:16: ". . . the assembly of the wicked have inclosed me: they pierced my hands and my feet."

Members of the Sanhedrin were proud of their familiarity with the scriptures. Surely they were aware of the prophecies

---

[59] *Scourge:* A vicious beating on the back that sometimes causes death.

concerning the method of Christ's death. According to their scriptures, the Messiah was to die by crucifixion. Yet the Sanhedrin seemed almost frantic to turn Christ over to the Roman leaders from whom he would receive that very death penalty. Their own actions were only further fulfilling the self-same prophecies that they blindly denied. For Christ's crucifixion was one more evidence that he was indeed the Messiah.

New Testament fulfillment—The unbridled crowd responded to the enthusiastic urging of the Sanhedrin and joined with their religious leaders as follows:

Matthew 27:22–23, 25: "Pilate saith unto them, What shall I do then with Jesus which is called Christ? They all say unto him, Let him be crucified. And the governor said, Why, what evil hath he done? But they cried out the more, saying, Let him be crucified . . . His blood be on us, and on our children."

Mark 15:13–14: "And they cried out again, Crucify him. Then Pilate said unto them, Why, what evil hath he done? And they cried out the more exceedingly, Crucify him."

Luke 23:21: "But they cried, saying, Crucify him, crucify him."

John 19:6: "When the chief priests therefore and officers saw him, they cried out, saying, Crucify him, crucify him . . . ."

John 19:15: "Away with him, away with him, crucify him."

But the New Testament scriptures do not stop with recording the crazed cries of the people—led by the Sanhedrin—to crucify Christ. All four Gospels also record the very fulfillment of the prophecy of his crucifixion:

Matthew 27:35: "And they crucified him . . . ."

Mark 15:24: "And when they had crucified him . . . ."

Luke 23:33: "And when they were come to the place, which is called Calvary, there they crucified him . . . ."

John 19:17–18: "And he bearing his cross went forth into a place called the place of a skull, which is called in the Hebrew Golgotha: Where they crucified him . . . ."

The lawmakers and judges who tried Christ could easily have secured witnesses to testify of the fulfillment of the above messianic prophesies and the many other prophecies of Jesus Christ, too numerous to detail here. The Sanhedrin, those who were learned in the law and serious students of the scriptures, should have been acutely aware of these prophecies. They should have recognized that many of the prophecies had indeed been fulfilled through Jesus the Christ.

TWELVE

THE ROMAN TRIALS

John 19:6 ". . . I find no fault in him."

Gethsemane's agony was a private suffering that the Lord endured alone, free of gossiping onlookers. Golgotha, however, would be a public display of cruelty and depravity. Although his beloved apostles could not stay awake at Gethsemane to keep watch with the Savior, they would now stand at the foot of his cross until it was finished. While no one could share in his ultimate sacrifice, many shared his long hours on the cross. Where the Garden had been quiet and heavy-eyed, the scene at the cross would invoke the heavens themselves to scream in pain and cry torrents for the Son of man. The blackness of the day is unparalleled, the suffering unequaled. But between Gethsemane and Golgotha loomed the Roman trials.

A Roman trial consisted of three distinct parts:

1. **The Accusation.** This had to be made by a private citizen. It was similar to someone filing a complaint in a court of law.

2. **The Inquiry.** This consisted of an inquiry, or examination, of the charge, including listening to and considering the accused's defense.

3. **The Decision.** This was the tribunal's judgment of the case.

Obviously, Roman trials were simpler and more streamlined than Hebrew trials, lacking the many rules and procedures that made Hebrew law a complex affair. But even the simple parameters of Roman law were abused when Christ was tried.

At the conclusion of the second Hebrew trial, which, like the first, was a travesty of justice, the whole Sanhedrin arose, "And when they had bound him [Jesus], they led him away, and delivered him to Pontius Pilate the governor" (Matthew 27:2). It was early in the morning that the Sanhedrin led him to the Roman hall of judgment. They had come for one reason: they wanted the Roman governor's approval to put Christ to death. The Sanhedrin itself did not hold that power.

Christ's trial before Pontius Pilate was held ". . . in a place that is called the Pavement, but in the Hebrew, Gabbatha" (John 19:13). Gabbatha in Hebrew or Aramaic is equivalent to lithostroton, which is a stone courtyard of the Hall of Judgment.

This Hall of Judgment was part of the palace in which Pilate resided when he was at Jerusalem.

Mark also referred to this Hall of Judgment as the Praetorium,[60] which is a Latin term for the hearing room portion of the Palace where the Roman Governor would transact public business. Pilate's judgment seat was located in the Praetorium. His seat was a raised platform similar to a throne from which, as governor, he sat in judgment.

This Hall of Judgment was located at the Fortress Antonia—a monumental military and governmental complex originally constructed by the Hasmoneans. It was re-constructed by Herod the Great on the northwest corner of the Temple. Herod renamed the Hasmonean Fortress the Antonia Fortress to honor his Roman friend Mark Anthony. The cohort of soldiers assisting in the arrest of Jesus was stationed at the Fortress to keep watch over the Temple Mount.

In an outward display of piety on this feast day, the members of the Sanhedrin ". . . went not into the judgment hall, lest they should be defiled . . . "(John 18:28).[61] Considering that the entire 24-hour period surrounding Gethsemane and Golgotha was replete with the Sanhedrin's cruelties, lies, illegalities, and even murder, it seems absurd that they now feared defilement and its consequence—being denied the Passover feast. That moment of waiting outside the judgment hall was laden with

---

[60] Mark 15:16

[61] The judgment hall was in the house (palace) of a Gentile, Pontius Pilate. If a Jewish person entered such a place on Friday, he would be considered unclean on Saturday, the Jewish Sabbath.

irony. After making a mockery of their own judicial system, those pious members of the Sanhedrin were too devout to enter the home of a gentile, or the palace of Pilate (where the judgment hall was located), on a feast day. No doubt even their Lord and Savior, in his confined condition could not fail to notice their game of hypocrisy.

But Pilate played the game. He had become acutely aware of how overly devout these Jewish leaders could be. He ". . . went out unto them, and said, What accusation bring ye against this man?" (John 18:29) The Jewish trials of Jesus had been illegally held without ever pronouncing a specific charge against Christ. At the end of the trial, the Sanhedrin had cried "blasphemy!" but they knew that such a charge would be meaningless to the pagan Pilate. Having all kinds of "gods," the Romans recognized no such crime as blasphemy. In fact, Roman leaders often declared themselves to be gods so that they would be worshipped after they died.

With no specific charge to offer, the Sanhedrin answered Pilate's question defensively: ". . . If he were not a malefactor, we would not have delivered him up unto thee" (John 18:30). Their response implies that they did not expect to be questioned on the matter of a charge. Since Pilate had likely cooperated with the arrest of Christ by allowing the assistance of Roman soldiers, the chief priests likely expected Pilate to condone their death penalty without question. But Pilate did not acquiesce to their desires. Possibly assuming that the charges brought against Jesus violate the Jews' own religious code, he replied, ". . . Take ye him, and judge him according to your law. The Jews therefore said unto him, It is not lawful for us to put any man to death . . . " (John 18:31). This reply further indicates that the real intent of the meeting with Pilate was to have their sentence of death approved and carried out by the procurator.

But Pilate's answer convinced the Sanhedrin that they would have to bring specific charges against Christ. After discussing it among themselves, ". . . they began to accuse him, saying, We found this fellow perverting the nation, and forbidding to give tribute to Caesar, saying that he himself is Christ a King" (Luke 23:2). This three-fold charge brought by the chief priest satisfied the first of the three parts of a Roman trial: the Accusation.

The three specific charges in the accusation against Christ were political, not religious, claiming he was in some way a threat to Rome and to Caesar's authority. But these charges were absurd. Christ did anything but pervert the nation; he was constantly admonishing his followers to be peacemakers and to serve and love one another. Christ did not oppose paying tribute, or taxes. And once, when Jesus perceived that the thousands he had just fed with five barley loaves and two fishes were anxious to make him a king, ". . . he departed again into a mountain himself alone" (John 6:15). Christ did not seek political power; he did not *want* to be king . . . not in an earthly sense. Nor had he criticized the Sanhedrin on political issues, only religious.

The first two charges from the Sanhedrin were of little significance to Pilate. As to Christ's perverting the nation, Pilate already considered the Jews perverse to the ways of Rome. And he must have considered Christ's "forbidding to give tribute to Caesar" to be idle rhetoric by grasping politicians, or perhaps he had even heard of Christ's powerful sermon to ". . . Render therefore unto Caesar the things which are Caesar's . . . " (Matthew 22:21). However, Pilate showed some concern that Christ claimed to be a king. He entered into the judgment hall where Christ was bound ". . . and called Jesus, and said unto him, Art thou the King of the Jews?" (John 18:33)

Again Christ's insightful response announced his unparalleled brilliance when he answered Pilate's question with one of his own: ". . . Sayest thou this thing of thyself, or did others tell it thee of me?" (John 18:34) Christ wanted to know who or what inspired Pilate's question—exactly what did Pilate mean? Had Pilate been speaking temporally or spiritually?

Pilate's response made it clear that his question concerned only temporal matters: ". . . Am I a Jew? Thine own nation and the chief priests have delivered thee unto me: what hast thou done?" (John 18:35)

Christ had the ability to answer life-threatening questions with the simplest truths: ". . . My kingdom is not of this world: if my kingdom were of this world, then would my servants fight, that I should not be delivered to the Jews: but now is my Kingdom not from hence" (John 18:36).

Pilate wanted to be certain, ". . . Art thou a king then? Jesus answered, Thou sayest that I am a king. To this end was I born, and for this cause came I into the world, that I should bear witness unto the truth. Every one that is of the truth heareth my voice" (John 18:37).

At this point Pilate, not recognizing that he stood before the embodiment of truth, asked the skeptical, oft-repeated question: ". . . What is truth?" (John 18:38) It is interesting that

Pilate should ask this question, for just a few hours earlier, Jesus had defined that very word. Only moments after instituting the ordinance of the sacrament, he told his apostles: ". . . I am the way, the truth, and the life: no man cometh unto the Father, but by me" (John 14:6).

And even earlier in his preaching, the Lord had taught his disciples how they could discover the *truth*: ". . . If ye continue in my word, then are ye my disciples indeed; And ye shall know the truth, and the truth shall make you free" (John 8:31–32).

Tragically, Pilate did not recognize truth—the divinity of, the very essence of, the Savior. However, he didn't seem guilty of malice towards Christ. He seemed even anxious to spare Christ's life and concerned that the trial be conducted fairly.

Pilate had now fulfilled the second part of Roman trial law—the Inquiry—questioning and examining the accused. He had asked Christ: "Art thou a king then?" and had given consideration to the defense: "My kingdom is not of this world."

After listening to Christ, Pilate rose from the judgment seat and proved that he was not concerned with the Sanhedrin's accusations against Christ when ". . . he went out again unto the Jews, and saith unto them, I find in him no fault at all" (John 18:38).

Pilate had rendered his judgment, and, thus, the third and final part of the Roman trial—the Decision—had concluded. Or should have. Since Pilate was the extension of Tiberius Caesar, his authority was absolute. When Pilate rose and pronounced the verdict, "I find in him no fault at all," it was an acquittal. Christ should have been let free. Case closed. Over. Done. Finished. Any future proceedings on those same charges would be illegal—as in trying a man twice for the same offense.

But Pilate's pronouncement of innocence caused much consternation among the chief priests, who were frantic for the blood of Christ. "And they were the more fierce, saying, He stirreth up the people, teaching throughout all Jewry, beginning from Galilee to this place" (Luke 23:5).

Hearing those words, Pilate saw a possible escape from this uncomfortable situation, for ". . . When Pilate heard of Galilee, he asked whether the man were a Galilean. And as soon as he knew that Jesus belonged unto Herod's jurisdiction, Pilate sent him to Herod, who himself also was at Jerusalem at that time" (Luke 23:6–7).

Pilate sent the bound Christ to Herod Antipas, tetrarch of Galilee. Only a short time earlier, when Jesus was preaching his parables, healing on the Sabbath, and crying repentance, ". . . there came certain of the Pharisees, saying unto him, Get thee out, and depart hence: for Herod will kill thee" (Luke 13:31). Christ's response hints at humor when he calls Herod "that fox"(Luke 13:32).

Herod Antipas was responsible for the beheading of John the Baptist and at one time had believed that Christ was John reincarnated.[62] In spite of Herod's guilt and possible fear of Christ, he was glad to have Christ sent to him because he had heard many stories about him, and ". . . he hoped to have seen some miracle done by him" (Luke 23:8).

"Then he [Herod] questioned with him [Jesus] in many words; but he answered him nothing" (Luke 23:9). Christ knew his rights and remained silent while ". . . the chief priests and

---

[62] Matthew 14:1–2; Mark 6:14–16; Luke 9:7–9

scribes stood and vehemently accused him" (Luke 23:10).[63] So Herod saw Christ face to face and spoke to him, yet never heard his voice.

Since Herod was visiting Jerusalem, and was not in Galilee, Christ was not within Herod's jurisdiction. Had the trial been held in Galilee, the situation would have been different. With Herod being both a Roman tetrarch and a king over the Jews, Christ could have been accused of both sedition *and* blasphemy. But ". . . Herod with his men of war . . . mocked him [Christ], and arrayed him in a gorgeous robe, and sent him again to Pilate" (Luke 23:11).

Because of the deference Pilate gave to Herod in sending him Christ, and the mutually shared experience of trying Christ, these two unscrupulous Roman leaders developed a friendship where before there had been enmity.[64]

When Christ returned from Herod and once again found himself standing before the Roman governor, Pilate's verdict remained unchanged. Pilate addressed the chief priest, the rulers, and the people who were gathered, telling them that both he and Herod found no fault in Christ. Perhaps sensing their unyielding hearts, Pilate sought a solution through a Jewish tradition that coincided with the Feast of the Passover. On this feast day, it was a common practice for the Roman governor to release one prisoner to the people as a token of mercy.

---

[63] This was in fulfillment of prophesy: "He was oppressed, and he was afflicted, yet he opened not his mouth: he is brought as a lamb to the slaughter, and as a sheep before her shearers is dumb, so he openeth not his mouth." (Isaiah 53:7)

[64] Luke 23:12

Pilate "... knew that the chief priests had delivered him [Christ] for envy" (Mark 15:10) and that Christ was guiltless, so he asked the Jewish audience, "... ye have a custom, that I should release unto you one at the passover: will ye therefore that I release unto you the King of the Jews?" (John 18:39).

In unison the "... chief priests and elders persuaded the multitude that they should ask Barabbas, and destroy Jesus" (Matthew 27:20). They "... cried out all at once, saying, Away with this man, and release unto us Barabbas ... " (Luke 23:18).

We learn from the writings of the Jewish historian Josephus, and from other sources, the surprising fact that Barabbas had the given name of Jesus. This ugly coincidence is further intensified by the fact that "Bar-Abbas" means "son of the father." In Hebrew, Bar means son, and Abba means father.[65] In the Garden of Gethsemane, Jesus prayed to "Abba, Father" (Mark 14:36).

It is almost diabolical that the incensed crowd before Pilate was choosing between Jesus, spiritual son of the father, and Jesus, physical son of the Father. Barabbas, like all mankind, was a spiritual son of God, while Christ was the literal, physical son of God. "This frightful coincidence was so repugnant to the Gospel writers that they are generally silent upon it."[66] The crowd did not appreciate the symbolic significance as they cried out for the release of Barabbas. The very fact that Christ was selected for crucifixion over Barabbas saved that wicked

---

[65] A personal, familiar term for father
[66] Chandler, 132.

man from being killed. And, within hours, Christ would save the whole world from the dismal prospect of mortality: physical death, the eternal separation of body and spirit.

When the inflamed crowd screamed for the release of Barabbas, Pilate rose from the judgment seat, indicating, according to Gentile tradition, that the trial had ended and no sentence would be imposed. Pilate's refusal to sentence the Savior is not surprising, since he had already declared that he found no fault in him. The rising of the governor announced the innocence of the accused, and at that point Christ should have been set free.

Then, standing by the judgment seat, Pilate performed the deed which would later bring him infamy. He performed a Jewish rite that symbolized innocence and freed the soul from innocent blood.[67] "When Pilate saw that he could prevail nothing, but that rather a tumult was made, he took water, and washed his hands before the multitude, saying, I am innocent of the blood of this just person: see ye to it. Then answered all the people, and said, His blood be on us, and on our children" (Matthew 27:24–25). Never was a verdict of guilty pronounced.

Just as the governor's rising from the judgment seat should have caused the release of Christ, the hand washing should also have released him. But the hand washing did not free Christ from the cross or release Pilate from the responsibility.

---

[67] According to Jewish law, if an unsolved murder had been committed, the elders of the city were required to slay a heifer, ". . . wash their hands over the heifer . . . and say . . . Our hands have not shed this blood, neither have our eyes seen it. Be merciful, O Lord . . . and lay not innocent blood unto thy people . . . ." (Deuteronomy 21:6–8)

Even if washing his hands would have cleared Pilate's guilt, he did it too soon, before his decree to scourge and then to crucify the Lord.

Because the timelines of the four Gospels vary slightly in the hours surrounding the crucifixion, it is impossible to give an exact, moment-by-moment account of the event. But at some point, Pilate's wife, Claudia, interrupted the trial by sending a warning to Pilate: "Have thou nothing to do with that just man: for I have suffered many things this day in a dream because of him" (Matthew 27:19). Pilate was not unsympathetic, and would gladly have yielded to her, but his past had now caught up with him. Too many times he had offended the Jews. Too many times they had appealed to Caesar, complaining of Pilate's injustices against the Jews. Pilate's previous, careless acts now made it difficult for him to follow his conscience in judging Christ.

Concerned by his wife's warning and by his own conviction that Christ was innocent of any crime, and knowing that Barabbas was a robber—even a murderer, ". . . Pilate answered and said again unto them, What will ye then that I shall do unto him whom ye call the King of the Jews?" (Mark 15:12) "But they cried, saying, Crucify him, crucify him. And he said unto them the third time, Why, what evil has he done? I have found no cause of death in him: I will therefore chastise him, and let him go" (Luke 23:21–22).

It seemed reasonable. If Barabbas were released, then Christ must be kept—and punished. Hoping that a severe chastising of Christ might satisfy the people, ". . . Pilate therefore took Jesus, and scourged him" (John 19:1).

The Gospels are almost silent on the scourging, the inhumane brutality that preceded the cross. Luke doesn't mention it at all. The other three are nearly as quiet: ". . . and when he had scourged Jesus . . . " (Matthew 27:26). ". . . when he had scourged him [Jesus] . . . " (Mark 15:15). And the above scripture: "Then Pilate therefore took Jesus, and scourged him" (John 19:1). Just a matter of a few words. But the painful torture of scourging could fill volumes.

Scourging (or flogging) was a legal preliminary to every Roman execution, and only women and Roman senators or soldiers (except in cases of desertion) were exempt. The usual instrument was a short whip (flagrum or flagellum) with several single or braided leather thongs of variable lengths, in which small iron balls or sharp pieces of sheep bones were tied at intervals. Occasionally, staves also were used. For scourging, the man was stripped of his clothing, and his hands were tied to an upright post (or sometimes between two posts). The back, buttocks, and legs were flogged either by two soldiers (lictors) or by one who alternated positions. The severity of the scourging depended on the disposition of the lictors and was intended to weaken the victim to a state just short of collapse or death. After the scourging, the soldier often taunted the victim.

As the Roman soldiers repeatedly struck the victim's back with full force, the iron balls would cause deep contusions, and the leather thongs and sheep bones would cut into the skin and subcutaneous tissues. Then, as the flogging continued, the lacerations would tear into the underlying skeletal muscles and produce quivering ribbons of bleeding flesh. Pain and blood loss generally set the stage for circulatory shock. The extent of blood loss may well have determined how long the victim would survive on the cross.[68] Often the victim died of the scourging.

The Roman soldiers became quite proficient in this manner of torture. It is believed that the soldier chosen to conduct the scourging would inflict as many as 39–40 lashes. After 10 blows the flogging would stop. At this time a soldier would complete a washing of the victims back with salt water from a basin on the side of the post. This application would slow the bleeding. Then a soldier would wipe the back of the victim with olive oil from another bowl on the other side of the post. This would soften the flesh for the next round of blows. The soldiers would sit and play a game between series of floggings. After a short while the scourging would continue.

It seems shocking that the scourging alone did not satisfy the soldiers' desire to inflict pain upon Christ. But after that savage beating, ". . . they stripped him, and put on him a scarlet robe. And when they had platted a crown of thorns, they put it upon his head, and a reed in his right hand: and they bowed the knee before him, and mocked him, saying, Hail, King of the Jews! And they spit upon him, and took the reed and smote him on the head" (Matthew 27:28–30). Depending on the size of the crown, the reed likely did not hit Christ directly on the head, but instead, hit the crown of thorns, pushing it deeper into the flesh of his skull. Christ's patient suffering through this awful

---

[68] Excerpts taken from William D. Edwards, MD; Wesley J. Gabel, MDiv; Floyd E. Hosmer, MS, AMI, "On the Physical Death of Jesus Christ," *Journal of the American Medical Association (JAMA),* March 21, 1986 — Vol 255, No. 11: 1455–1463.

torment foreshadows his endurance through the more hideous spectacle of torture that awaited him.

After the scourging and the crown of thorns, Pilate announced, "Behold, I bring him forth to you, that ye may know that I find no fault in him. Then came Jesus forth, wearing the crown of thorns, and the purple robe. And Pilate saith unto them, Behold the man!" (John 19:4–5).[69] With blood dripping from his back and head, the Redeemer of all mankind humbly stood before his own people.

But that innocent blood dripping from his body did not satisfy the Sanhedrin. "When the chief priests therefore and officers saw him, they cried out, saying, Crucify him, crucify him . . . " (John 19:6).

It is incomprehensible that these words of death and horror would be escaping the lips of people who had only days earlier shouted out words of praise and adulation, including "Hosanna, blessed be the King." But for the most part, this crowd did not include the same people. The crowd assembled at Pilate's palace courtyard was comprised of the chief priests, scribes, and Pharisees, and such people as they could persuade to come and join them. This was the day of the Feast of the Passover, one of the most sacred of Jewish holidays. It is logical to assume that most Jews and their visitors were at home, preparing for the sacred feast.

But in spite of the crowd's bloodthirsty demands, Pilate again affirmed his own belief that Christ was innocent: ". . . I find no fault in him" (John 19:6). The Jews responded: ". . . We have a law, and by our law he ought to die, because he made himself the Son of God" (John 19:7). Pilate, a weak man and easily swayed, had put himself in a hard position. He had already declared that he found no fault in Christ, he had been warned by his wife that Christ was a just man, and now he heard that Christ was possibly the Son of God! Pilate took Jesus back into the judgment hall to question him more. But Christ would not answer him.

Finally, Pilate reminded this already beaten and bloody man that, as governor, he had the power of life and death over Christ. He could order Christ's crucifixion. It must have been an amazing scene. Pilate with his alleged power, wondering at Christ's unwillingness to respond. The Christ, seemingly in a point of incredible weakness, with his piercing crown and his oozing blood. But from his gentle lips came the majestic proclamation: ". . . Thou couldest have no power at all against me, except it were given thee from above . . . " (John 19:11). Powerful words from one in such an apparent powerless position.

But Pilate recognized in Christ something that the angry crowd outside the judgment hall did not, "And from thenceforth Pilate sought to release him . . ." (John 19:12).

It was at this point that the Jews pronounced their most frightening argument for the crucifixion of Christ. To Pilate's proposal of releasing Christ they cried out, ". . . If thou let this man go, thou art not Caesar's friend: whosoever maketh himself a king speaketh against Caesar"(John 19:12). It was a clever rebuttal, adding great pressure to Pilate, a direct representative of Tiberius Caesar—the paranoid emperor who had killed 52 people because he suspected they might want to take over his kingdom. Both Pilate and the Sanhedrin were well aware of Pilate's tenuous standing with Tiberius Caesar.

If Pilate let Christ go and word got back to Caesar that Christ had claimed to be a king, it might be the end of Pilate himself. Fearing Caesar more than Christ, ". . . he [Pilate] brought Jesus forth, and sat down in the judgment seat . . . .and he saith unto the Jews, Behold your King! But they cried out, Away with him, away with him, crucify him. Pilate saith unto them, Shall I crucify your King? The chief priests answered, We have no king but Caesar" (John 19:13–15). "And they were instant [Greek: *urging*] with loud voices, requiring [Greek: *demanding*] that he might be crucified. And the voices of them and of the chief priests prevailed" (Luke 23:23). "Then delivered he him therefore unto them to be crucified. And they took Jesus, and led him away" (John 19:16).

It was not what Pilate had wanted. Throughout the trial, he had been emphatic in his defense of Christ's innocence. There are at least ten references found within the four Gospels that record Pilate's defense of the Savior:

"I find no fault in him": (Appears 5 times) Luke 23:4; Luke 23:14; John 18:38; John 19:4; John 19:6

". . . this just person": (Appears once) Matthew 27:24 (In Matthew 27:19, *Claudia* refers to "this just man.")

"What evil hath he done?" (Appears 3 times) Matthew 27:23; Mark 15:14; Luke 23:22

"I have found no cause of death in him." (Appears once) Luke 23:32

In addition to declaring Christ's innocence throughout the Roman trials, Pilate made four distinct maneuvers to avoid the responsibility of crucifying Christ. First, Pilate had tried to return Christ to the Sanhedrin. He had instructed, ". . . Take ye him, and judge him according to your law . . . " (John 18:31). Second, Pilate had sent Jesus to be judged by Herod. Third, Pilate had offered to free Jesus during the traditional releasing of a prisoner during Passover. And fourth, he had hoped that chastising (presumably the scourging) the innocent would satisfy the bloodthirsty Jews, making a crucifixion unnecessary.

When Pilate saw that strict justice for Christ would threaten his position, he reluctantly and shamefully gave way to the demands of the Jews, sending Jesus to his death on the cross. Pilate should have followed his first inclinations and dismissed the case . . . but was not strong enough to carry out the correct decision.

THIRTEEN

THE CRUCIFIXION

Luke 23:34 ". . . Father, forgive them . . . "

Gethsemane's drops of blood had dried. The illegal trials had concluded. The awful scourging had, at last, abated. But ahead of Christ lay the dusty road to the cross. His tormentors, relentless and savage, mocked him, somehow unsatisfied with the pain they knew awaited at Golgotha, at the crucifixion: "And when they had mocked him, they took off the purple from him, and put his own clothes on him, and led him out to crucify him" (Mark 15:20).[69] When they left the hall called

---

[69] Crucifixion was of Phoenician origin, adopted by Rome. But even Herod in all his cruelty did not resort to this mode of execution. Edersheim, 583–584.

Praetorium, the soldiers compelled a man, Simon, a Cyrenian, who happened to be passing by to bear the cross for Christ.[70] It was an awesome responsibility and, somehow, a glorious gift— to carry the cross upon which Christ would die for all mankind.

Following Christ down this dusty road was ". . . a great company of people, and of women, which also bewailed and lamented him" (Luke 23:27). Along the way, perhaps as the weary cross-bearer stumbled under his load, Christ picked up the cross for himself, and ". . . bearing his cross [Christ] went forth into a place called the place of a skull, which is called in the Hebrew Golgotha" (John 19:17).

The place of the skull, Golgotha, and Calvary name the place where our Savior took his last mortal breath. At about 9 a.m., upon reaching the foreboding location, Jewish women provided Christ the customary draught of cheap wine or vinegar medicated with myrrh to deaden consciousness, to lessen the pain of the death Christ was about to suffer through crucifixion. "And they gave him to drink wine mingled with myrrh: but he received it not" (Mark 15:23). While the drink was probably taken freely by most to whom it was offered, Christ would not drink it "because . . . He needed to face the moment of death with his full faculties."[71]

The four Gospels give virtually no detail about the physical process of crucifixion, just the same three words: "they crucified him." But they do tell that Christ hung between two thieves and that ". . . Pilate wrote a title, and put it on the cross. And the writ-

---

[70] Luke 23:36

[71] Edersheim 589–590

ing was, JESUS OF NAZARETH THE KING OF THE JEWS" (John 19:19). Since the place where Jesus was crucified was not far from the city, many Jews passed by and read the sign that was written in Hebrew, Greek, and Latin. The Sanhedrin were outraged by the sign on the cross of Christ. "Then said the chief priests of the Jews to Pilate, Write not, The King of the Jews; but, that he *said*, I am King of the Jews" (John 19:21).

Pilate's unquestioned power had taken a heavy loss that day. He had not wanted to send Jesus to his crucifixion. To this request to change the sign, it is easy to imagine Pilate smugly answering the chief priests: ". . . What I have written, I have written" (John19:22). We can't know Pilate's purpose in the wording of Christ's sign. Perhaps he was getting revenge. Perhaps he believed Christ really was a spiritual king of sorts. No matter Pilate's purpose, his sign was true. The humble Nazarene hanging on that cross was, in fact, "JESUS OF NAZARETH THE KING OF THE JEWS."

It was time.

Crucifixion probably first began among the Phoenicians. Alexander the Great introduced the practice to Egypt and Carthage, and the Romans appear to have learned of it from the Carthaginians. Although the Romans did not invent crucifixion, they perfected it as a form of torture and capital punishment that was designed to produce a slow death with maximum pain and suffering. It was one of the most disgraceful and cruel methods of execution and usually was reserved only for slaves, foreigners, revolutionaries, and the vilest of criminals. Roman law usually protected Roman citizens from crucifixion, except perhaps in the case of desertion by soldiers.

It was customary for the condemned man to carry his own cross from the flogging post to the site of crucifixion outside the city walls. He was usually naked, unless this was prohibited by local customs. Since the weight of the entire cross was probably well over 300 pounds (136 kg), only the crossbar was carried. The patibulum, weighing 75 to 125 pounds (34 to 57 kg), was placed across the nape of the victim's neck and balanced along both shoulders. Usually, the outstretched arms then were tied to the crossbar. The processional to the site of crucifixion was led by a complete Roman military guard, headed by a centurion. One of the soldiers carried a sign (titulus) on which the condemned man's name and crime were displayed. Later, the titulus would be attached to the top of the cross. The Roman guard would not leave the victim until they were sure of his death.

At the site of execution, by law, the victim was given a bitter drink of wine mixed with myrrh (gall) as a mild analgesic. The criminal was then thrown to the ground on his back, with his arms outstretched along the patibulum. The hands could be nailed or tied to the crossbar, but nailing apparently was preferred by the Romans.

Next, the feet were fixed to the cross, either by nails or ropes. Although the feet could be fixed to the sides of the stipes or to a wooden footrest (suppedaneum), they usually were nailed directly to the front of the stipes.

Since no one was intended to survive crucifixion, the body was not released to the family until the soldiers were sure that the victim was dead. The actual cause of death by crucifixion was multifactorial and varied somewhat with each case, but the two most prominent causes probably were hypovolemic shock and exhaustion asphyxia. Other possible contributing factors included dehydration, stress-induced arrhythmias, and congestive heart failure with the rapid accumulation of pericardial and perhaps pleural effusions. Crucifracture (breaking the legs below the knees), if performed, led to an asphyxic death within minutes. Death by crucifixion was, in every sense of the word, excruciating (Latin, *excruciatus,* or "out of the cross").[72]

While the four Gospels give us little information concerning the act of crucifying, Bruce R. McConkie offers vivid detail of Christ being nailed to the cross:

"The three crosses were laid on the ground—that of Jesus, which was doubtless taller that the other two, being placed in bitter scorn in the midst. Perhaps the crossbeam was now nailed to the upright, and certainly the title, which had either been borne by Jesus fastened round His neck, or carried by one of the soldiers in front of Him, was now nailed to the summit of His cross. Then He was stripped of His clothes, [he may have been spared of full exposure in deference to Jewish sensibilities . . .[73]] and then followed the most awful moment of all. He was laid down upon the implement of torture. His arms were stretched along the cross-beams; and at the centre of the open palms, the point of

---

[72] Edwards, 1455–1463

[73] Edersheim, 584

a huge iron nail was placed, which, by the blow of a mallet, was driven home into the wood. Then through either foot separately, or possibly through both together as they were placed one over the other, another huge nail tore its way through the quivering flesh. Whether the sufferer was also bound to the cross we do not know; but, to prevent the hands and feet from being torn away by the weight of the body, which could . . . 'rest upon nothing but four great wounds,' there was, about the center of the cross, a wooden projection strong enough to support, at least in part, a human body which soon became a mass of agony."[74]

The actual nailing to the cross would cause excruciating pain . . . yet there were unfathomable *hours* ahead. One wonders at the coldheartedness of the soldiers who ". . . when they had crucified Jesus [nailed him to the cross], took his garments, and made four parts, to every soldier a part . . . " (John 19:23). And because they could not divide his coat without ruining it, they threw dice for it, a game of chance played for our Savior's coat.

And yet, for those soldiers it was not enough. The mockery. The smiting. The spitting. The scourging. The crown. The nailing. It was not enough. ". . . they that passed by reviled him . . . saying . . . save thyself. If thou be the Son of God, come down from the cross. Likewise also the chief priests mocking him,

---

[74] Bruce R. McConkie *The Mortal Messiah Book 4* (Salt Lake City: Deseret Book Company,1981) 211–215.

with the scribes and elders, said, He saved others; himself he cannot save. If he be the King of Israel, let him now come down from the cross, and we will believe him" (Matthew 27:39–42).

And he was suffering for the very sins they had committed and were committing against him . . . patient throughout their abuse.

As he hung on the cross, our Lord and Savior Jesus Christ spoke seven times. His words are interesting and insightful, ever setting the example for all mankind to follow.

The first, and probably most famous, message is found only in the Gospel of Luke: "Then said Jesus, Father, forgive them; for they know not what they do. And they parted his raiment, and cast lots" (Luke 23:34). This quote from Jesus was directed at the soldiers who had just nailed him to the cross and were now dividing up his clothes and playing a game of chance for his coat. He watched them. Nailed to that rough wooden cross, blood dripping from hands and feet, lifted higher than any other being on Calvary, the Savior was able to observe the men who had inflicted the grotesque wounds in his hands and feet. And he asked the Father to forgive them. Was ever a better lesson taught? The submissiveness and humility in his prayer for those Roman soldiers who were gambling for his coat, ". . . Father, forgive them; for they know not what they do . . . " (Luke 23:34) take on new meaning and importance when we recognize the gross violations of rules and procedures of law perpetrated by his tormentors.

Atop that hill, Christ was flanked by two thieves who were divided in their opinion of him. One mocked him; the other believed in him and pleaded, ". . . Jesus, Lord, remember me when thou comest into thy kingdom"(Luke 23:42). The second message spoken by Christ was his response to that thief: "And Jesus said unto him, Verily I say unto thee, Today shalt thou be with me in paradise" (Luke 23:43).

John is the only Gospel writer who records the third comment that Christ uttered from the cross. Considering what Christ had endured for the previous 15 hours, the sentiment of his statement is even more meaningful. First, Christ had not slept for some 30 hours. The previous evening he had experienced the mental agony and suffering of Gethsemane—where pain had caused him to bleed from every pore. Dragged from the Garden like a criminal, he was exposed to three different illegal Jewish questionings or trials perpetrated by angry opponents. He experienced further humiliation in the Roman hall of judgment and the examination before Herod. He was mocked, struck, and spit upon throughout the night. The scourging, the crown of thorns, the carrying of the cross, and finally, the excruciating pain of the nails biting into his tender flesh must have left him nearly senseless. Yet after all of that, Christ's third comment was one of loving concern for his mother, who was standing by the cross: He gave the assignment to care for his mother to His beloved disciple, John. "When Jesus therefore saw his mother, and the disciple standing by, whom he loved, he saith unto his mother, Woman, behold thy son! Then saith he to the disciple, Behold thy mother! And from that hour that disciple took her unto his own home" (John 19:26–27).

Jesus had now been hanging on the cross for about three hours—from approximately 9 a.m. to noon. He was about halfway through his ordeal on the cross, for he would continue to suffer another three hours before he succumbed. During those final three hours, the scriptures record that ". . . there was a darkness over all the earth . . ." (Luke 23:44).

"And about the ninth hour Jesus cried with a loud voice, saying . . . My God, my God, why hast thou forsaken me?" (Matthew 27:46) The Lord's fourth comment, then, was to announce his feeling of being utterly alone. "In that bitterest hour the dying Christ was alone, alone in a most terrible reality. That the supreme sacrifice of the Son might be consummated in all its fullness, the Father seems to have withdrawn the support of His immediate Presence, leaving to the Savior of men the glory of complete victory over the forces of sin and death."[75]

Shortly before the end, during the three hours of darkness, Jesus spoke his shortest message from the cross. Two words. Two little words that reaffirmed his physical parentage: ". . . Jesus knowing that all things were now accomplished, that the scripture might be fulfilled, saith, I thirst" (John 19:28). And to this dying man someone offered a sponge soaked in vinegar.

The sixth and seventh comments from the cross were probably uttered at the same time. John records: "When Jesus therefore had received the vinegar, he said, It is finished: and he bowed his head, and gave up the ghost" (John 19:30).

Luke, alone, makes reference to Christ's return to his Father: "And when Jesus had cried with a loud voice, he said,

---

[75] Talmage, 661

Father, into thy hands I commend my spirit: and having said thus, he gave up the ghost [Greek: *expired, ceased breathing, or died*]" (Luke 23:46).

It was finished.

FOURTEEN

THE RESURRECTION

Matthew 28:6 "He is not here: for he is risen . . . "

All four Gospel authors acknowledge that Christ "yielded up" or "gave up" the ghost.[76] Our Savior *gave* up his life. As he showed with the fig tree, *he had the power over life itself*. Matthew, Mark, and Luke all record that just before "giving up the ghost" Jesus cried with a loud voice.[77] Indeed He was uttering a great cry of triumph, for he had flawlessly finished his awesome responsibility that had been foretold by the prophets of old.

---

[76] See Matthew 27:50, Mark 15:37, Luke 23:46, John 19:30

[77] See Matthew 27:50, Mark 15:37, Luke 23:46

The great mission of that babe born in a stable and laid in a manger was gloriously fulfilled.

At the moment Jesus gave up his life, ". . . behold, the veil of the temple was rent in twain from the top to the bottom; and the earth did quake, and the rocks rent; And the graves were opened; and many bodies of the saints which slept arose, And came out of the graves after his resurrection" (Matthew 27:51–53). A centurion and others nearby who had been watching Jesus became afraid, ". . . saying, Truly this was the Son of God" (Matthew 27:54).

Even after he was dead, prophecies about Jesus continued to be fulfilled. John detailed one of them. Crucifixion can take many hours. Sometimes, in order to speed up the process and to make sure that the man was dead, soldiers would break the legs of a person on the cross. If he hadn't died yet, shock or suffocation would cause immediate death. Soldiers did break the legs of the two thieves who hung on either side of Christ. "But when they came to Jesus, and saw that he was dead already, they brake not his legs" (John 19:33). This fulfilled the prophecy foretold in Psalms 34:20: "He keepeth all his bones: not one of them is broken."

John's next words seemed unbelievable at the time: "But one of the soldiers with a spear pierced his side, and forthwith came there out blood and water" (John 19:33–34). John then emphatically writes another verse to make sure we believe him: "And he that saw it bear record, and his record is true: and he knoweth that he saith true, that ye might believe" (John 19:35). John seems adamant in his effort to make us believe what he wrote.

It is interesting, with our current medical understanding, that what John observed could indeed have happened. Due to the beatings and scourging Christ had received shortly before being nailed to the cross, he had lost a significant amount of blood. Because his body weight was suspended by his arms, his lungs became compressed, and breathing became difficult. Due to the shallow breathing, his lungs began to collapse in small areas. In order to exhale, he had to shift the weight of his body by pushing up on his feet. Each time he did so, his raw back rubbed the rough wood of the cross, initiating yet more bleeding.

With that excruciating combination of difficulty in breathing and loss of blood, Christ was not receiving the needed oxygen that naturally would be delivered throughout the body. As his breathing became more labored, his heartbeat grew faster and faster—trying to compensate for the lack of oxygen. Fluid built up in his lungs. Christ was already dead when the soldier pierced his side, releasing the blood and water.

Though many causes contributed to the death of Jesus Christ, the two most obvious were cardiorespiratory failure and cardiac rupture. It is the likelihood of a cardiac rupture that whispers that Christ died of a broken heart.

By Jewish law a man could not remain on the cross through the Sabbath. So it was not surprising that "When the even was come, there came a rich man of Aramathea named Joseph, who also himself was Jesus' disciple: He went to Pilate, and begged [Greek: *asked for, requested*] the body of Jesus. Then Pilate commanded the body to be delivered. And when Joseph had taken the body, he wrapped it in a clean linen cloth, And laid it in his own new tomb, which he had hewn out in the rock: and he rolled a great stone to the door of the sepulchre, and departed" (Matthew 27:57–60).

The Gospel of Mark adds a comforting word, declaring that Joseph of Arimathea bought *fine* linen in which to wrap the Lord.[78] *Fine* linen. Though his work was done, though his spirit was free, it is a comfort that his torn and beaten body was laid to rest in fine linen by those who loved him.

While the other three Gospel writers record that Joseph of Arimathea recovered the body with the permission of Pilate, John alone adds that Nicodemus assisted Joseph by bringing about 100 pounds of mixed spices, myrrh and aloes. "Then took they [Joseph and Nicodemus] the body of Jesus, and wound it in linen clothes with the spices, as the manner of the Jews is to bury" (John 19:40).

"Now the next day . . . the chief priests and Pharisees came together unto Pilate, Saying, Sir, we remember that that deceiver said, while he was yet alive, After three days I will rise again. Command therefore that the sepulchre be made sure until the third day, lest his disciples come by night, and steal him away, and say unto the people, He is risen from the dead: so the last error shall be worse than the first. Pilate said unto them, Ye have a watch: go your way, make it as sure as ye can. So they went, and made the sepulchre sure, sealing the stone, and setting a watch" (Matthew 27:62–66).

---

[78] Mark 15:46

Saturday, April 8, A.D. 34
(Jewish Sabbath)

"And they . . . rested the sabbath day according to the commandment" (Luke 23:56). On this day, Christ's body lay in the tomb.

High Day, April 9, A.D. 34

John is the only Gospel writer who comments on "high day." He mentions it somewhat as an aside, even in parentheses: ". . . (for that sabbath day was an high day) . . . " (John 19:31). It is interesting that he should make that observation. Perhaps he did so to help bring clarity to the words Christ uttered in Matthew 12:40: "For as Jonas was three days and three nights in the whale's belly; so shall the Son of man be three days and three nights in the heart of the earth." Those are Christ's own words, stating that he would be in the tomb three days and three nights. Yet it seems Christ spent only two nights in the tomb—Friday and Saturday nights. Until we consider "high day."

One theory suggests that "high day" was the manner in which the Jews allowed for what we have labeled "leap year." That extra day every fourth year that is inserted to allow for the inexact number of days that the earth revolves around the sun. Instead of inserting it at the end of February, as our present calendar system does, the Jews of that time tacked the extra day that accumulated every four years onto one of their favorite holidays of the year—the Feast of the Passover. They considered it a second sabbath of the week. If the weekend of

Christ's crucifixion did indeed include a "high day," then that would account for the third day in the tomb, of which Jesus prophesied.

Just as on their regular sabbath of the day before, on this "high day" also, Christ's body would have lain in the tomb. And they would have ". . . rested the sabbath day according to the commandment" (Luke 23:56).

Sunday, April 10, A.D. 34
Easter Sunday, the Resurrection

"And when the sabbath was past, Mary Magdalene, and Mary the mother of James, and Salome, had brought sweet spices, that they might come and anoint him" (Mark 16:1). The women were concerned that there might not be someone available to roll away the large stone that covered the entrance to the tomb. But they need not have worried: ". . . behold, there was a great earthquake: for the angel of the Lord descended from heaven, and came and rolled back the stone from the door, and sat upon it" (Matthew 28:2). The seal to the tomb had been broken, the stone rolled away, and the guards who had been placed there at the request of the chief priests were gone. "And the angel . . . said unto the women, Fear not ye: for I know that ye seek Jesus, which was crucified" (Matthew 28:5). Of course they were fearful! Three humble women who had come on a tearful but innocent errand to tend to the body of their beloved Jesus. They had not expected an angelic visitation. But then the most glorious words ever spoken on this earth rang out as the angel continued, "He is not here: for he has risen, as he said . . . " (Matthew 28:6).

Though they did not yet understand the eternal importance of the message, the women were instructed to ". . . go quickly, and tell his disciples that he has risen from the dead; and, behold, he goeth before you into Galilee; there shall ye see him: lo, I have told you. And they departed quickly from the sepulchre with fear and great joy; and did run to bring his disciples word" (Matthew 28:7–8).

The word spread. In an effort to discredit the reality of the resurrection, ". . . when they [the chief priests] were assembled with the elders, and had taken counsel, they gave large money unto the soldiers, Saying, Say ye, His disciples came by night, and stole him away while we slept. And if this come to the governor's ears, we will persuade him, and secure you. So they took the money, and did as they were taught . . . " (Matthew 28:12–15).

The resurrection of our Lord and Savior Jesus Christ was well documented. According to his own words, Christ had risen. Many testified of his personal, post-mortal appearance to them:

- Mary Magdalene (Matthew 28:1–9; Mark 16:9; John 20:13–17)
- The other Mary (Matthew 28:1–9)
- The 10 or 11 disciples (Thomas missing) (Matthew 28:17; Mark 16:14; Luke 24:33–36; John 20:19–23)
- Second visit to the 11 disciples (John 20:26–29)
- Third visit to the 11 disciples (John 21:14)
- Cleopas and another on the road to Emmaus (Luke 24:13–31)
- Simon Peter (Luke 24:34, 1 Corinthians 15:5)
- Cephas (I Corinthians 15:5)
- The Twelve Apostles (I Corinthians 15:5)

- More than 500 brethren at once (1 Corinthians 15:6)
- James (I Corinthians 15:7)
- Second visit to the Twelve Apostles (I Corinthians 15:7)
- Paul the Apostle (I Corinthians 15:8)

Just as he had promised, Christ had risen and become the first fruits of them that slept. Without his resurrection and his atonement for human sin, our lives would be empty and dark, void of hope for a future life with him and our Father in Heaven. Because Christ was resurrected, all mankind shall live again. Every person ever born will enjoy that amazing gift the Savior freely offers. The Apostle Paul beautifully and simply teaches the power of Christ's resurrection in I Corinthians 15:20–22, "But now is Christ risen from the dead, and become the firstfruits of them that slept. For since by man came death, by man came also the resurrection of the dead. For as in Adam all die, even so in Christ shall all be made alive."

The illegal actions of the Jewish leaders brought about the death of Christ . . . but those actions also brought about the completion of his resurrection and atonement. The trial of Christ *was* unfair. It *was* illegal. And that is one of the great ironies of the ages. It was the illegal trial of Christ that opened for all mankind the precious gifts of mercy and fairness. Sadly, there is only one thing in this life that one can count on to be fair—and it will be brilliantly fair for everyone.

After this life in which we all experience moments of great sorrow and unfairness, we will each be judged by Christ, who has suffered all things with us, who knows and understands our hearts and desires. And without exception, for at least that one moment in our lives, we can all count upon perfect fairness. *Christ's judgment of us will be fair*, unbiased, just. And as we kneel before him and observe the marks on his feet, we will all realize that our very salvation was made possible because of the *illegal*, unfair trial that Christ—our Lord and Savior, the Redeemer of all mankind—endured in Judea.

Suggested Reading List

Asch, Sholem. *The Nazarene.* New York: G.P. Putnam & Sons, 1939.

Bishop, Jim. *The Day Christ Died.* New York: Harper & Row Publishers, 1957.

Blessing, William Lester. *The Trial of Jesus.* Denver: House of Prayer for All People, Inc., 1955.

Brandon, S.G.F. *The Trial of Jesus of Nazareth.* New York: Stein & Day Publishers, 1968.

Chandler, Walter M. *The Trial of Jesus Vol. 1 and 2.* New York: The Empire Publishing Co., 1908.

Edersheim, Alfred. *The Life and Times of Jesus the Messiah.* Grand Rapids, Michigan: Wm. B. Eerdmans Publishing Co., 1971.

Edwards, William D., MD; Wesley J. Gabel, MDiv; and Floyd E. Hosmer, MS, AMI. "On the Physical Death of Jesus Christ." *Journal of the American Medical Association (JAMA)* March 21, 1986, Vol. 255, No. 11.

Farrar, Frederic D.D., F.R.S. *The Life of Christ.* New York, A.L. Burt, 1874.

Geikie, Cunningham, D.D. *The Life and Words of Christ.* New York: D. Appleton and Company, 1894.

Maranon, Gregorio. *Tiberius, the Resentful Caesar.* New York: Duell, Sloan & Pearce, 1956.

McConkie, Bruce R. *The Mortal Messiah Book 4.* Salt Lake City: Deseret Book Company, 1981.

Michell, John. *The Temple at Jerusalem: a Revelation.* Boston: Weiser Books, 2001.

Nielsen, Donna. *Reading Between the Lines: Mining the Treasures of Scripture.* Provo: Onyx Press, 2004.

Penrod, Everett. *Pilate: Victor or Victim?* Kearney: Morris Publishing, 2002.

Radin, Max. *The Trial of Jesus of Nazareth.* Chicago: The University of Chicago Press, 1931.

Richards, John E. *The Illegality of the Trial of Jesus.* New Orleans: Louisiana Printing Co, Ltd., 1914.

Talmage, James E., *Jesus the Christ.* Salt Lake City: Deseret Book Company, 1962.

Thompson, George W. *The Trial of Jesus.* Brooklyn, New York: The Bobbs-Merrill Company, 1927.

Whiston, William, Translator. *Josephus Complete Works.* Grand Rapids, Michigan: Kregel Publications, 1960.

ABOUT THE AUTHOR

Steven W. Allen is a lawyer, an author, a professional speaker, and an avid reader who loves to travel to historical sites. He is currently in his third decade of legal practice with his expertise in estate planning, asset protection and the inter-generational transfer of wealth. He has given over 1,000 presentations in several states on these subjects. He is a member of the National Speakers Association, the State Bar of Arizona, the National Lawyers Association, and the National Association of Elder Law Attorneys.

For nearly 20 years, Steve has spoken to numerous groups and organizations about "The Illegal Trial of Christ from a Lawyers Standpoint." Steve takes a lawyer's view of the most famous trial of all time and gives the reader a deeper understanding of the injustices that led to Christ's unwarranted death. He has inspired thousands of people as he brings law and religion together to reveal the illegalities of Christ's trial. His presentations have been so well received that many of his students prompted him to write this book.

Steve is also a patriot. His passion about the founding fathers and the creation of our country inspired him to write the book *Founding Fathers – Uncommon Heroes*. He reveals little-known facts and foibles that bring George Washington, Benjamin Franklin, John Adams, Thomas Jefferson, Patrick Henry, and James Madison to life. It's companion, *Give Me Liberty and Other Quotes from Great American Leaders* is the perfect gift book.

Steve lives with his wife, Linda, in Mesa, Arizona and enjoys spending time with his five children and seven grandchildren.

FREE E-NEWSLETTERS
BY STEVEN W. ALLEN

Patriotic Salutes

Don't miss it! This entertaining newsletter is filled with interesting stories about America and its leaders. Learn little-known facts, and dispel fallacies as you enlighten your mind and develop a greater respect for our country. The newsletter highlights national patriotic holidays (and some rather unusual holidays—such as National Waffle Day). This newsletter is fun for the whole family.

To subscribe to this FREE newsletter, please visit *www.UncommonHeroes.us*

Secrets of Wealth Preservation

Sign up now! Join a very select group of subscribers who will have valuable secrets of wealth preservation regularly unveiled to them through this FREE newsletter! This upbeat, informative newsletter offers just what its title says and dispenses tips and hints to help protect, maintain, and increase your assets. You'll wonder how you ever managed without it!

To subscribe to this FREE newsletter, please visit *www.LegalAwareness.com*

The Illegal Trial of Christ
From a Lawyer's Standpoint

For nearly 20 years, Steven Allen has inspired audiences with his unique twist on the greatest story ever told. From his professional perspective, he entwines law and religion and opens the eyes of even the most learned scriptorian. Allen clearly details the procedures of Roman and Hebrew law and the astonishing truth of the most famous trial in history. The trials (yes, there was more than one) were held in the wrong place, at the wrong time, by the wrong people, with the wrong witnesses. And those are just a few of the numerous illegalities revealed in this captivating presentation. The Illegal Trial of Christ from a Lawyer's Standpoint is beyond educational . . . it is inspiring! It will offer you a deeper understanding of the events surrounding Christ's crucifixion and instill a deeper appreciation for his magnanimous act.

Leadership—as Taught by Our Founding Fathers

In all of history, there have been few leaders with the amazing qualities of George Washington, Benjamin Franklin, and Thomas Jefferson. Steven Allen brings these historical characters to life as he shares glimpses of their character and personality. By offering pieces of their life story, Allen helps his audience discover how these historical leaders were superb examples of decisiveness, wisdom, character, and follow-through. And perhaps most important of all, Allen teaches his audience how to emulate Washington, Franklin, and Jefferson and to become top-ranking leaders in every aspect of their life.

continued on next page

You Can't Take it with You . . .
So How Are You Going to Leave it Behind?

Steven Allen is a master at turning legalese into an understandable and entertaining presentation. As an estate planning attorney of 30 years, he has amassed an enviable amount of knowledge on the subject. And countless experiences with clients over those 30 years provide him innumerable real-life examples that help his audience fully understand his critical financial counsel. Everyone leaves Steven Allen's lecture with a penetrating understanding of wills, trusts, property ownership, and business entities. Armed with this vital information, participants will be better able to protect their assets from taxation and lawsuits.

To find out when Steven Allen
will be lecturing in a city near you, go to
www.SteveAllenSpeaks.com

To schedule a speaking engagement,
please contact Steven Allen at:
Steven W. Allen, JD
1550 E. McKellips Road, Suite 111
Mesa, AZ 85203
Phone: 480-644-0070
E-mail: Steve@StevenAllen.com

Founding Fathers – Uncommon Heroes

In *Founding Fathers—Uncommon Heroes*, respected author Steven W. Allen gloriously brings to life the American Revolutionary heroes: from visionary attorney John Adams to sage philosopher and inventor Ben Franklin; from idealistic author, statesman and architect Thomas Jefferson to the Father of Our Country, the gallant General George Washington; and from inspiring speaker and lawyer Patrick Henry to the persistent and studious Father of the Constitution, James Madison. Steven Allen's most stirring achievement, *Founding Fathers—Uncommon Heroes,* reveals how philosophers became heroes, how ideas became their weapons, and how a scattered group of weak colonies became the United States of America through the lives and actions of these most uncommon heroes.

www.UncommonHeroes.us

Founding Fathers – Uncommon Heroes
Now Available on Audio CD!
www.UncommonHeroes.us

Give Me Liberty,
And Other Quotes From
Great American Leaders

A compilation of quotes from great American leaders that provoke thought and laughter. These tidbits of wisdom and witticism from George Washington, Benjamin Franklin, Thomas Jefferson, John

Adams, James Madison, Patrick Henry and Thomas Paine are timeless—in fact, they are needed now more than ever. Learn what these incredible men had to say about freedom, character, achievement, government, and history in this volume that is both educational and entertaining.

www.GiveMeLibertyQuotes.com

Coming soon:
You Can't Take It With You . . .
So How Are You Going To Leave It Behind?

Who doesn't have questions about estate planning? As an estate planning attorney with over 30 years of experience, Steven Allen shines a brilliant light of clarity on the mystifying subjects of wills and trusts (and the difference between them). He also explains how to protect assets, how to set up a business entity, and much more. Using wit and humor, Allen is a master at turning legalese into easily readable, understandable and practical information. This book teaches you the most effective way to leave your assets to your loved ones . . . and not to Uncle Sam.

www.HowToLeaveItBehind.com

To purchase any of Steve's products visit:
www.LegalAwareness.com

CHECK BOOKSTORES EVERYWHERE OR ORDER HERE.

Toll-Free: 1-800-733-5297

Secure online ordering at *www.legalawareness.com*

Book Title	Quantity	Price
The Illegal Trial of Christ ISBN: 1-879033-31-3 Hardcover $19.95		$
Founding Fathers: Uncommon Heroes ISBN: 1-879033–76-3 Softcover $19.95		$
Founding Fathers: *Uncommon Heroes on CD* ISBN: 1-879033-75-5 Audio book on 6 CDs $24.95		$
Give Me Liberty ISBN: 1-879033-12-7 Hardcover $12.95		$
You Can't Take It With You So *How Are You Going To Leave It Behind?* ISBN: 1-879033-97-6 Softcover (available May 2005) $19.95		$

Shipping: USA: $4.95 for first item; add $2.00 for each additional book AZ residents please include 7.8% tax	Shipping		$
	Total		$

Please Print:

Name _____

Company_____

City/State/Zip_____

Phone _____E-mail (optional) _____

Credit card # _____Expires: _____

Please sign_____

Mail to:
Legal Awareness Series, Inc.
1550 E. McKellips Rd., Suite 111
Mesa, AZ 85203

To book Steven W. Allen for your conference or event
call 1-800-733-5297 or email *Steve@StevenAllen.com*